KOI VARIETIES

JAPANESE COLORED CARP-NISHIKIGOI

BY DR. HERBERT R. AXELROD

Dedicated to my dear friends, Dr. Arthur and Dr. Judy Topilow, whose assistance and constant encouragement led to this book.

I wish to thank Takeshi Yokoyama for his assistance in translating the captions from the Japanese.

Distributed in the UNITED STATES by T.F.H. Publications, Inc., One T.F.H. Plaza, Neptune City, NJ 07753; in CANADA to the Pet Trade by H & L Pet Supplies Inc., 27 Kingston Crescent, Kitchener, Ontario N2B 2T6; Rolf C. Hagen Ltd., 3225 Sartelon Street, Montreal 382 Quebec; in CANADA to the Book Trade by Macmillan of Canada (A Division of Canada Publishing Corporation), 164 Commander Boulevard, Agincourt, Ontario M1S 3C7; in ENGLAND by T.F.H. Publications Limited, Cliveden House/Priors Way/Bray, Maidenhead, Berkshire SL6 2HP, England; in AUSTRALIA AND THE SOUTH PACIFIC by T.F.H. (Australia) Pty. Ltd., Box 149, Brookvale 2100 N.S.W., Australia; in NEW ZEALAND by Ross Haines & Son, Ltd., 18 Monmouth Street, Grey Lynn, Auckland 2, New Zealand; in SINGAPORE AND MALAYSIA by MPH Distributors (S) Pte., Ltd., 601 Sims Drive, #03/07/21, Singapore 1438; in the PHILIPPINES by Bio-Research, 5 Lippay Street, San Lorenzo Village, Makati Rizal; in SOUTH AFRICA by Multipet Pty. Ltd., 30 Turners Avenue, Durban 4001. Published by T.F.H. Publications, Inc. Manufactured in the United States of America by T.F.H. Publications, Inc.

CONTENTS

会場搬入

第19回全日本総合錦鯉品評会の幕開け。
会場準備のための静から動をカメラで記録した。

SCENES FROM THE 19TH ALL-JAPAN NISHIKIGOI SHOW
Held in Tokyo (Haneda) area in 1987.

晴天の設営当日

一番の到着車

鯉を待つ会場内

受付風景①

受付風景②

受付風景③

受付風景④

1. WHAT ARE NISHIKIGOI?

Colored carp all descended from the wild carp which probably originated in eastern Europe through to Persia. Wild carp are called "Koi" in Japanese. Later on the term "Koi" was applied to all carp, both the wild and the colored. The Japanese now have a special word for wild carp which is "Magoi." Colored and inbred Magoi are called Koi. Those Koi which have been bred for color are called "Nishikigoi." Many Japanese use the word "Koi" to indicate wild carp. However, the term "Koi" has taken on a secondary meaning in most of the world. "Koi," to most of the English speaking world, means the colored carp which the Japanese refer to as the "Nishikigoi."

THE ORIGINS OF NISHIKIGOI

There seems to be no question that Nishikigoi or Koi had their origin in China. I made a trip to China in 1988 to complete my studies of the origin of Chinese colored carp and found that the Chinese did indeed feature red and white colored carp, as well as the wild carp, in many of their artistic productions. I found that a series of carp stamps was issued in China starting in 1897. I also found that centuries old works of Chinese ivory and wall hangings also featured colored carp. I was fortunate in being able to photograph many of the Chinese decorations featuring carp. Wood

Two Doitsu carp photographed by the author in Berlin Aquarium, Berlin, Germany. These two old carp are supposed to be 20 years old and weigh 5 kg (11 pounds). The Mirror Carp has the scales basically along the dorsal fin of the fish. The carp in the background is fully scaled. These carp have completely different physiques than the Chinese or Japanese carps from which the koi ostensibly descended. These Doitsu carp were used for cross-breeding with Oriental carps early in the Twentieth Century.

Besides owning statues and carvings of koi, an omen of good luck is to catch a koi by yourself and eat it! Thus many Chinese carvings depict lucky fishermen catching a carp. This one, from the Republic of China, is made of jade. Photo by Dr. Arthur Topilow.

carvings and porcelain are popular manifestatio of the love and respect the Chinese have for car

Delving into the history of carp in China, I d covered quite a bit of folk lore dealing with th carp. During the pre-Republican period in Chin the accumulation of wealth was usually associate with one's ability to get an official appointment government. Only in this way could the tax co lector be warded off. Every large family, therefor did everything possible to fall under the umbre protection of a Member of the Mandarin. It w common for people who were associated wi Mandarin to share their wealth with him on a vo untary basis. This was the only way that the pe son was able to acquire wealth without havi most of it taxed away. In order to become a mer ber of the Official Government, it became nece sary to have a good education and to pass certa tests. Scholarship in those days was the only w to get a Civil Service job. During the Civil Servi Examination one of the common gifts from th family to the candidate was an effigy of a car Wealthy families presented the carp in ivory or valuable stone; while others made it out of po tery, clay, wood, or semi-precious stones. Som times even a live carp was given. The reason th the carp was used to signify help for the candida was the legend of the carp who used every bit his energy to pass up the rapids to become dragon.

The supernatural powers of the carp are evi denced in many Chinese works of art. This monkeypod wood carving depicts a carp vir tually walking on water in its effort to scale waterfalls and rapids to reach its goal in life . . . a suitable place to spawn.

Don't think of all dragons as evil, as the Chi-
[se] conception of a dragon was very mixed.
[o]st dragons are benevolent and even though
[th]ey are frightening, they can be pleasant and pro-
[tec]tive. This is basically the same feeling that the
[or]dinary Chinese person had for the Mandarins. A
[Ma]ndarin could indeed be powerful, ugly, and
[am]bitious, but at the same time this power could
[be] converted to charitable and helpful causes.

The legend goes that a great carp swam up the
[Ye]llow River to the T'ung Kuan Rapids and be-
[ca]me a dragon. He became a good dragon and
[the] Chinese have used the carp to represent the
[tok]en of how if a young person works hard and
[ke]eps striving, they will be able to achieve any-
[thi]ng and do good for the world. Something like
[the] English version of the tortoise and the hare.
[Ev]en though the tortoise moves very slowly, and
[the] rabbit was very fast, the fact that the turtle kept

This magnificent carving from mahogany wood was made in Taiwan, Republic of China, in the early 1980's. It is carved from a single block of mahogany and depicts the ancient story of the valiant struggle of Chinese carp "walking on water" in their quest to reach the waiting plump female in order to spawn.

[Thi]s ancient Chinese vase is decorated with carp. The vase is
[abo]ut 250 years old (circa 1750) and has a value of about
[$5,]000 (3,000 pound Sterling).

plodding on hour after hour and day after day while the hare had a rest, eventually fell asleep, enabled the tortoise to win the race.

It is still a custom during New Year's Day that the carp is given as a symbol of how to achieve success through hard work. The carp was especially given as a stimulant to students to help them pass their school examinations.

This wooden carving of a koi was discovered by the author in China in 1988. It was given as a gift to a student as a token of industriousness and determination. The wood is monkeypod, a very hard Pacific area wood often used for carving.

This stamp was issued in 1897 and is a single example of a series of stamps issued between about 1897 and 1902 which featured the Chinese carp. This is further evidence of the Chinese people's early love for the colored carp.

The term "Nishikigoi" was created from the word "Nishiki" which refers to Chinese brocaded silk. Thus this more prominently establishes a connection between colored carp and their origin in China. It is believed that the Chinese called these fish "brocaded carp."

More expensive statues and good-luck tokens are even made of solid gold resting on a stand of precious stones imbedded in a solid golden pedestal. Koi statues like this are made to order in the Republic of China for wealthy patrons.

CARP IN JAPAN

The first records of carp in Japan were four around the time of the birth of Christ, about 2,00 years ago. No one seems to know when the fir colored mutants from wild carp were found in J pan, but it seems fairly certain that they were ir ported from mainland China. China is also the o gin of fancy goldfish and it seems that th breeding of fish was an early achievement of th Chinese people.

According to Japanese legend, the earliest co ored carp were red and called "Higoi." At th same time that the Higoi were produced, whi carp showed up on the scene. These fish we called "Shirogoi." There seems to be some refe ence, also many hundreds of years ago, to blackish or a grayish red koi which is calle "Asagi." No one really has any accurate recor or illustrations of these fish, but they do appear the literature. Earliest references for carp wer "Higoi" or red carp and "Irogoi" for colored car Sometime in the early 1800's breeders started cross the Higoi and the Shirogoi to produce a re and white spotted carp which was called "Ko haku." These were produced in Miigata Prefe ture, approximately 175 miles west of Tokyo.

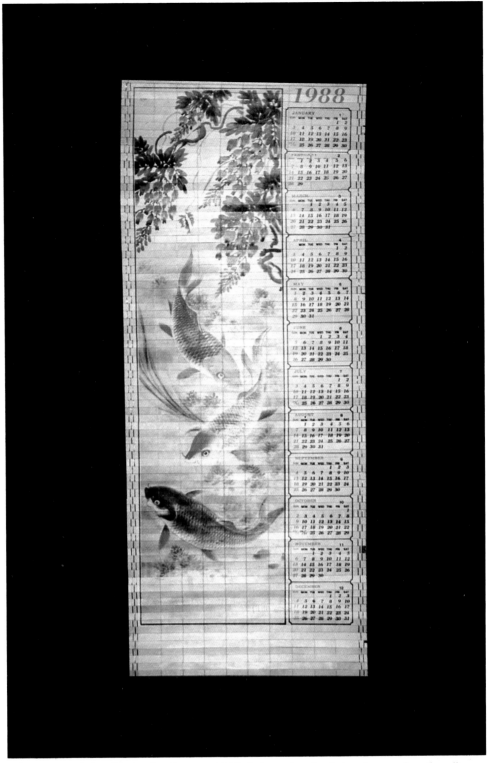

A Chinese-English calendar for the year 1988. It is made of split bamboo and easily rolls up. Painted by hand (there are cheaper copies printed by machine or silk screening), this calendar features a copy of an old Chinese print showing wild carp, golden koi and red koi. The Chinese are as infatuated with koi as are the Japanese, and their folklore is laden with stories of heroic carp swimming up impossible waterfalls and rapids to prove that where there is a will, there is a way!

This magnificent bit of Chinese art shows a breeding scene in a koi pond. Beautiful water lilies and lotus decorate the scene, while two kittens watch the scene playfully. The koi depicted are typical ancient Chinese carp which are wild colored, white, or red-and-white. This painting is done on transparent single-thread silk. It has been valued at $50,000 (30,000 pounds Sterling).

This ivory carving, made in China, shows a Japanese fisherman carrying koi off to the market to sell for food. The Chinese do not breed colored carp for resale as food . . . neither do the Japanese now. But I did eat koi when I was living in Japan between 1950 and 1953.

This is a closeup of the spawning koi shown on the Chinese silk print. They almost look real, don't they? This painting was done in old China.

Upper fish: This is a White Doitsugoi or German carp. It is a Mirror Carp because it has a naked body except for the lines of scales along its dorsal edge. The lower fish is a magnificent Striped Doitsugoi because it has scales along the dorsal edge plus scales along the lateral line. The color variety is Shusui which means "autumn sky" which is a reference to sunset (the red belly of the fish).

These Kohaku koi were inbred in an effort to produce perfect specimens according to Japanese standards of taste at that time.

It was not until about 100 years later, early in the 1900's, when German carp were imported from Europe. These carp were gray and lacked any color, but they did have a very interesting scale development. It would probably be more accurate to say that the German carp had a lack of scale development since they had only a few large scales. These carp were called "Doitsu." This is the Japanese equivalent of the word "Deutsch" which means "German" in the German language.

There were three kinds of German carp which are distinguished. The "Kagamigoi" is also known as the "Mirror Carp." This carp has just a few small scales along the dorsal line on both sides of the dorsal fin. The "Kawagoi," known as the "Leather Carp," has scales along the dorsal edge of the fish as well as along the lateral line. The "Yoroigoi" which is called the "Striped" is a Kawagoi and Kagamigo combined. In 1904, the first crosses between the German carp and the Japanese carp were successfully made. The resulting fish were called "Doitsu Nishikigoi."

2. HOW KOI BECAME POPULAR

The interest in Nishikigoi seems to be centered around Ojiya City, Miigata Prefecture. It was 1914 when Emperor Hirohito who was then the Crown Prince and interested in fishes, attended a fish exhibition in Ueno Park in Tokyo. The Crown Prince was so interested in Koi shown there he was able to acquire eight of them and brought them into the palace grounds. When I visited with Emperor Hirohito in 1951, he told me that specimens from this initial 8 were still living and that most of the Koi to be found around the palace grounds were produced by these eight fishes.

It was the Emperor Hirohito himself then who really was responsible for making the Koi so popu-

One corner of the moat surrounding the Imperial Palace of Emperor Hirohito in Tokyo, Japan. The moat is filled with nishikigoi, which have been a favorite of the Emperor since he was a Prince.

This is why koi are popular. They are eating out of my wife's hand!

This old Japanese print by Utamaro is entitled "Carp in Brocade" or "Koi in Nishiki-e." It is one of thousands of illustrations in which the Orientals have portrayed carp. On the other hand, I can't recall of the carp figuring in any significant Western art.

Both sides of the koi are marked differently. Even the tail is marked differently on each side.

This lovely Chinese ivory koi pair belongs to Dr. Judith Topilow, Ocean, New Jersey. This koi is a Kohaku showing unrealistic markings from a Japanese point of view.

A top view compares two koi ivory figures made in Communist China, where the laws about using ivory are different from Western laws of conservation and protection of wild animals.

A head-on-view of the Kohaku ivory koi from China shows the Hi (red) spot, which belongs on the head far forward on the nose or snout of the fish.

This is an imitation Aka-Bekko. The black Sumi mark is dull and uninteresting, even on an ivory figurine. You can barely make out the black marks on the bottom of the caudal peduncle and top of the skull.

Comparing the Aka-Bekko with the Kohaku we can observe differences in structures which are meaningful for nishikigoi enthusiasts but not for artlovers (as long as they don't keep koi).

The snout on the Aka-Bekko is more realistic, but the lips and snout are distended in an artificial manner. In any case, this is the way a Chinese ivory carver sees koi.

This side of the Aka-Bekko is marked differently from the other side.

The Chinese people in Hong Kong honor the carp in many ways. This 1988 stamp was issued to commemorate the affection Chinese have for carp. This stamp shows a Chinese lantern imitating a koi. Candles are put inside the lanterns, and they are placed outside the residence of the person who wishes good luck.

The carp is memorialized in China by almost every kind of art form. The porcelain industry has produced this flower urn made to look like a carp jumping up a waterfall. Legend has it the carp eventually became a good dragon.

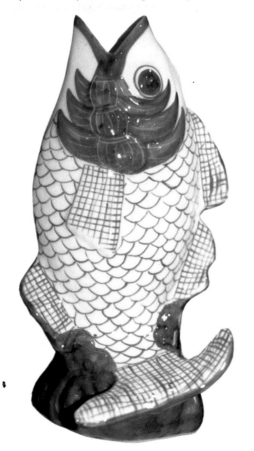

lar in Japan. And it was soon thereafter that contests were held by the farmers around Ojiya to see who produced the most beautiful fish. At that time, Koi were spawned at the time that the rice was planted. Rice in the area of Ojiya is only one crop a year and it is planted in the Spring when it is ideal for the Koi to spawn. The farmers then put the Koi eggs out in the rice paddies where they would hatch. The young gobbled up the mosquito larvae, which seem to have been horrendous at that time.

As the Koi got larger they were fed discarded silkworm cocoons which were a by-product of the silk manufacturing processes. Even to this day discarded cocoons are used as Koi food in many parts of Japan.

Most of the Koi which were bred and which did not turn out to be too colorful were used as food, and carp are still an important part of the diet all around the world. My grandmother told me that in Poland during the time of the occupation of the Russians, in the late 1800's and early 1900's, that live carp were available from stores for the celebration of different holidays. The carp were brought home, wrapped in cloth, and were prepared after they died. In 1987 when I visited Poland, I checked out this ancient custom and found that the custom was not so ancient! Live carp are still sold around Christmas and Easter and people lucky enough to buy them take them home and put them in the refrigerator till they die and then they are served as the highlight of a festive meal.

THE KOI HOBBY VS. THE KOI BUSINESS

When I visited Yoshida in 1960, Yoshida being one of the largest Koi farmers at the time, he slaughtered a prize Koi right in front of me, cut off its head and in a very beautiful ceremony selected choice parts of the Koi for me to eat. It was not one of my favorite meals, but there was nothing I could do but accept it graciously. Thus, the colored Nishikigoi actually were a by-product of fish farmers in Miigata Prefecture who were basically raising Koi for food. It was only with constant inbreeding that certain varieties were able to breed true. To this day, almost no varieties breed 100% true, though certain varieties such as Kohaku, Taisho Sanshoku, Showa Sanshoku, Asagi, Shusui, Bekko, Utsuri, and solid color varieties like Yamabuki Ogon, breed pretty true when identical fish are bred to each other. However, most of the carp are cross-bred.

The favorite fish of the Japanese is still the red and white Koi known as Kohaku. This red and white fish always seems to be the grand prize winner in competitions. Western taste, especially in the United States and Britain, seems to tend to the more colorful fish. However, with the establishment of more and more Koi societies, it seems that the rare varieties of Koi are being inbred and Japanese standards are being applied.

Unfortunately, there is conflict between the standards used by dealers and those used by breeders.

Top quality carp demand a huge price! While I was in Japan in January, 1988, I saw a carp trade hands for approximately 2,000,000 Yen. At the time, this was equal to about U.S.$15,000 or about 10,000 Pounds Sterling. I was told that no high quality carp are sold to Americans but they are available if Americans would like to buy them. Most large Koi dealers are willing to sell fish one at a time by mail order. At the present time, they send photographs of the fish with prices written on the back of the photograph as well as a description and sometimes a pedigree. The individual can then buy an individual fish which is sent by air.

The dealers' association breaks Koi up into thirteen sizes and thirteen color groups. The sizes go from Size 1 which is a fish 6" or 15 cm long and increases by 5 cm with each category. Thus, the first size is up to 6" or 15 cm, the second size is 15 to 20 cm or 6 to 8 inches, the third size is 20 - 25 cm all the way up to the thirteenth size which is 70 cm or about 28".

COLOR VARIETIES

There are 13 color groupings. Most Koi lovers will refer to these groupings as the Japanese do, in the Japanese language. Dealers want the Koi to be grouped according to every five centimeters in their length so they could have many different sizes to sell and because the larger the koi the more time and food has gone into grow it. However, hobbyists only want to have five or six size groups because when you think about the groupings with 13 sizes and 13 colors in each size, you can imagine how many categories there will be (169) in a Koi show.

The Kamihata Koi Farm in Japan produces more koi than any other koi farm in the world. It has an irrigation and overflow system which prevents fish escaping or native fishes entering. These concrete-lined ponds are unique. Most farms have dirt pools.

To produce this book and to keep it up-to-date in future editions, an agreement was entered into between the author (left), Mr. Yokoyama (center), and Mr. Kamihata. Yokoyama-san produces an annual yearbook showing the winners of the All-Japanese National Koi Competition which is held annu-

ally near the old Tokyo airport in Haneda, Japan. Mr. Kamihata is the owner of the largest nishikigoi farm in the world, makes the best-selling brand of koi food under the trade name of HIKARI, and is President of the Koi Farmers of Japan Association. The publisher of this book, T.F.H. Publications, has agreed to publish authentic and authoritative books on koi for the English-reading people of the world. The author, Dr. Herbert R. Axelrod, brought the first nishikigoi to America in the 1940's and bred them at his fish farm in Florida. He has maintained an active connection with Japanese nishikigoi breeders since 1950 when he lived in Japan.

A close-up of the koi painting on the Chinese wall hanging. This silk painting was presented to Mr. S. Kamihata by the autho
during a visit to Japan in 1988.

18

In the early 1960's the Koi societies decided to have classifications according to annual growth. That is, Year 1 or Size 1 was fish up to 18 cm; Size 2 is between 18 and 36 cm; Size 3 between 36 cm and 48 cm; Size 4 was 48 cm or larger. However, the Supreme Aquarium Society which is called Airinki finally made a compromise classification. The first size was 18cm, the second size up to 25cm; the third size up to 35cm; fourth size to 45cm; fifth size to 55cm; sixth size to 65cm; seventh size to 75cm; and eighth size over 75cm.

Size is a very important characteristic. If two koi are equal in all other characteristics, the larger one will get the better prize. Considering all of this, what dealers want to use to put a value on their fish and what the hobbyist wants to use for fish shows, it does not seem like a truce will last very long.

English and American dealers that I visited in early 1988 value their carp basically by size, when colors are more or less equal. The quality of koi available in the United States and Britain are extremely poor compared to the carp which are shown in Japan. I was very lucky to be able to obtain photographs of hundreds of champion carp. These photographs will be found scattered throughout the book, through the courtesy of Messrs. Kamihata and Yokoyama.

Another view of the Kamihata Koi Farm which shows much smaller ponds where breeding and experimentation take place.

Kamihata, aside from being the largest producer of fine nishikigoi in the world, is also a major producer of fancy goldfish. This is a photograph of his hatchery. He also imports and distributes tropical aquarium fishes throughout Japan.

Dr. Judith Topilow, a practicing physician in New Jersey, poses alongside an ancient Chinese wall hanging silk painting of two koi. Photo by Dr. Arthur Topilow.

3. THIRTEEN BASIC VARIETIES

KOHAKU

Kohaku are by far the most popular color variety in Japan. They are also the oldest color variety, inasmuch as they were the original Koi coming from China. The Kohaku is a white Koi with red markings. This color combination is extremely appealing to Japanese. If you recollect, the Japanese flag is a red circle on a white background. At every Koi show which I visited during many trips to Japan, it was always a Kohaku which won. I lived in Japan (1950-1952) and every prize went to Kohaku.

The Japanese have an expression that "you start keeping Nishikigoi with Kohaku and you end keeping the Nishikigoi with Kohaku." What this means is that Kohaku is basically an easy fish to breed and yet it is very difficult to get a supreme specimen. The same, of course, is true for tropical fish lovers when they can raise guppies. Everybody can breed guppies, though very few can breed championship quality guppies.

The Kohaku was officially named about 1889 or 1890 in Japan, but it was named several hundred years before that in China. It started to be protected and appeared in Koi shows in Ojiya City about 1917. According to Kamihata more than 50% of the Koi produced in Japan are this variety. Kohaku represents 40% of the fishes entered into competition. Kohaku are usually bred and produced by breeding two Kohaku together. However, many three color Koi, Taisho Sanke, which are basically white fish with mostly red and a little bit of black, also produce two colored carp or Kohaku.

There are many different varieties of Kohaku. Some Kohaku are all white and only have red lips; some only have a red stomach, while some only

1. Kohaku. 2. Taisho Sanke. 3. Showa Sanke, or just Showa for short. 4. Asagi. 5. Hi Jusui (red Shusui). 6. Tancho Sanke. 7. Hi Utsuri (red on black). 8. Shiro Utsuri (white on black). 9. Bekko. 10. Shiro Bekko (black spots on a white base). These photographs are found in the Prospectus from Kamihata. Dealers, importers and hobbyists are invited to write to Mr. Tsuda, Kamihata Fish Industries, 1330 Amado-cho, Chiba City 281, Japan. Their Fax number is (472)57-5344 (add country code and international access code). Inquiries should only be for commercial purposes.

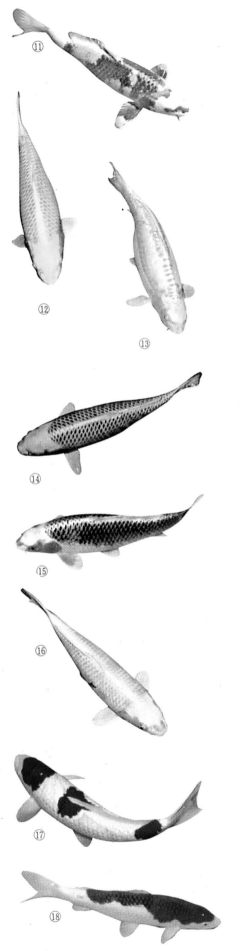

This large Kohaku was photographed by the author in Hawaii in 1962. The Hi spot didn't appear on the top of the head where it belongs, instead it came out on one cheek! Otherwise it is an interesting koi.

have red on the gill plates. These are not show quality specimens. The Japanese have definite standards for what a Kohaku should look like. In the first case, the red should be a very deep red. In the second case, the white should be snow-white. One of the faults of the Kohaku is that instead of snow-white skin, the skin tends to be yellowish. This is definitely not a good characteristic of a Kohaku. Sometimes small black spots will appear on the skin. This is also a sign of a poor specimen.

Beside the white being very white and the red, which the Japanese call Hi, being very dark, the pattern of the red is very, very important. There are Japanese names for all kinds of different patterns. Kohaku which have small red markings are called "Komoyo." Kohaku with large markings are called "Omoyo." Omoyo are definitely preferable and are much more valuable than Komoyo. The main reason that large red markings are valuable in young fish is that as they grow older the markings become more meaningful when they are large than when they are small and the larger fish develop a much more balanced look.

11. Hikari Utsuri variety known as Kin Shiro Utsuri (metallic silverish black). 12. Hikari Muji variety known as Yamabuki Ogon (yellow gold). 13. Hikari Muji variety known as Nezu Ogon (grey gold). 14. Purachina Ogon (platinum) which is also a variety classified under Hikari Muji. 15. Kujaku Asagi (metallic peacock), a variety of Hikari Moyo. 16. Hariwake ,the platinum-bodied yellow-patterned nishikigoi, is also a variety of the Hikari Moyo. 17. The Kin-Ginrin variety known as the Ginrin Kohaku, is a two-color red/white fish with metallic scales. 18. Koromo variety Aigoromo is a Kohaku-type two-color with a bluish cast over the red areas. These are expensive fish!

This is a prize-winning Kohaku.

The Japanese evaluate Koi by looking at them from the top. Imagine that the dorsal fin represent part of the mid-line along the back by which Ko are measured. The red color should basically bal ance along this imaginary center line along the back.

Another point of interest as far as Koi lovers ar concerned is whether the red markings on the back are connected or are separated. When the markings are connected from the head to the ta in a continuous pattern, they are given speci names by the Japanese. You can best visualize th by looking at the captions under the various pho tos which accompany this text. The main thing understand is that the pattern should be beautifu The pattern should also be meaningful. Sometime when there are three or four large separate mar ings called "steps," they remind Japanese peopl of the stones they put in their garden stepping ov the muddy ground to get into the house witho getting their shoes dirty. Usually a continuous re pattern from head to tail is boring and is not ve valuable. If, however, the red is jagged rather tha straight, this is then called an "Inazuma," whic means lightning shape. The pattern must be irre ular to be attractive, and must be interesting. Ps chologists who ask us to interpret ink blotches ca have a great time getting interpretations fro some of the designs on the backs of Koi!

The concept of balance of these markings something which comes from experience. Fish ar judged by this balance. There are no two judg in the world who would probably grade each fis exactly the same way. The same is true of ca shows, dog shows, and horse shows. Howeve with dogs, cats, and horses, as well as with man birds, they breed almost 100% true. Thus, if yo take true white horses and breed them togethe you would expect to get all white horses as a re sult. However, it is quite possible, for example that if you breed two silver poodles together, yo might get a black poodle, a silver poodle, or brown poodle. This is exactly what happened t my silver poodle when I bred her to another silve poodle. Genetics of Koi is very complex, too

Thus, when Koi are bred to each other, you ar not exactly sure what is going to come out, but th Kohaku color, that is red blotches on white, fairly consistent though the pattern of these blo ches, the location and the intensity and size ar variable and do not necessarily result from th quality of the parents.

According to present standards, Kohaku mu have a red marking on its head. As a matter o

During the past, Kohaku red was usually restricted to the area on top of the body, that which would be visible from the top in a small pond. However, as more and more American, British, and European taste become involved in Koi, side markings and belly markings are becoming more desirable. The Japanese, in order to please their customers, have decided to accept red markings along the sides and on the belly, too.

Under all circumstances, Kohaku must have red markings reaching to within one inch of the beginning of the tail. The red patterns should have very distinct edges and should not fade away into pinks. Also, there should not be any separate red markings as small as a single scale. So far, we are only talking about the color pattern of red and white.

Along with color patterns, intensity of color, and size, there are physical considerations such as lack of color on the fins, as well as the shape of the body, the way the fish swims, the shape of the head, etc. The best way to appreciate these color

...ancho, the Japanese crane. The red Hi spot on the head of ...e crane served as the model for the Tancho nishikigoi ...andard.

...act, there is even a variety of Kohaku which is a ...eparate grouping known as the "Tancho." A Tan-...ho Kohaku is a fish which is pure white and has ...nly a red spot on its head. These fish are very ...aluable but the white must be very, very white ...nd the red must be very intense and almost circu-...ar in most cases.

The ideal red (called Hi) on the head is U-...haped spreading over the head without covering ...he eyes. Under all circumstances, the white col-...ring should predominate over the mouth and ...ips.

I have had many Kohaku which were abso-...utely adorable. They had what would amount to ...'lipstick." The small red markings on the lips ...have a Japanese name called "Kuchibeni." Kuchi-...beni are a despised color in Japan because ladies ...of the night wear very heavy lipstick to designate ...heir occupation. This is very distasteful to Japan-...se. So to conclude, the best Kohaku would have ...he head covered as much as possible with a deep ...red Hi in the shape of a circle or a U, but the red ...Hi must not disturb the eyes, gill covers, or lips.

Prize-winning Tancho Kohaku.

patterns and physical characteristics is to look at the accompanying photographs where the quality of the Kohaku are demonstrated and the qualities and faults pointed out.

The philosophy of Japanese judges in judging thousands of Koi at a Koi show is peculiar. Normally they go through all of the Koi first and eliminate those which have faults. Then they keep weeding down fish until they have fish with fewer faults. When they finally reach the bottom of the barrel, they have fish which only have good traits and these are the ones which are prized.

American and British judges, however, take a different approach. They look for good qualities of the fish and if the fish has an excellent Hi spot on its head, has very good conformation, an excellent pattern, and good swimming behavior, then slight imperfections are overlooked. Koi which are eliminated in the first round in Japan might very well win a top prize in America or Britain. Who is to say who is right?? The Japanese defend their position by saying slight imperfections should be bred out of the fish and therefore imperfections should disqualify fish from ever becoming champions. You have both sides of the story, and you know enough now to decide to which philosophy to which you would like to adhere.

This old scientific drawing shows an Oriental carp, *Cyprinus carpio*, from which nishikigoi have descended. It looks nothing like the European carp known by the same scientific name. They might well be two different fish.

KOHAKU DEGENERATES

Often Kohaku parents produce single color fish. The plain white Koi called "Shiromuji," and "Okamuji" which are plain red Koi, are really Kohaku with a color missing. These are considered of very poor value and are usually disposed of as soon as their color becomes apparent, very young in their life. Actually, in the English speaking world, these are very valuable Koi and very interesting.

Of course, there are Doitsu Kohaku which have different scalations. There are also "Goten-zakura." The Goten-zakura Koi have a peculiar pattern on the scales which is rather round resembling a bunch of grapes or a pinecone. However, other Koi which have the pinecone look are actually designated as pine needles. Zakura is also spelled with an "S," Sakura, which refers to cherry blossoms. Sakura is also the name of a city outside of Tokyo. Sakura is a very favorite flower of the Japanese so a fish with the name of Goten-zakura would be very valuable. Goten-zakura which have a gold ring or edging around each scale are called "Kin-zakura." They are extremely valuable.

TAISHO SANKE

These might also be referred to as Taisho Sans-hoku depending upon how you read the Japanese characters. Basically "Taisho" refers to the period in Japan from 1911 to 1924 which was the period prior to control of the Emperor Hirohito. Thus Taisho Sanke refers to three colored fish which made its appearance during the Taisho era. There are different authors who date the Taisho era between 1911 and 1912, and from 1924 to 1926. It does not really matter, except that the first illustration of the Taisho Sanke is dated in 1914. The Taisho Sanke is essentially a Kohaku to which black splashes are added. The color should be very deep. The white should be snow-white, the red should be blood-red, and the black should be as black as possible. There should be no black on the head, or at least no black on the front part of the head which would be basically in front of the eyes. It is generally acceptable for "Sanke" which is the short name for "Taisho Sanke," to have some black streaks on their paired fins.

A variety of Sanke known as "Aka Sanke" is basically red fish with small blotches of black and white. The Sanke fish represent about ⅓ of the varieties seen in various competitions. Show qualifi-

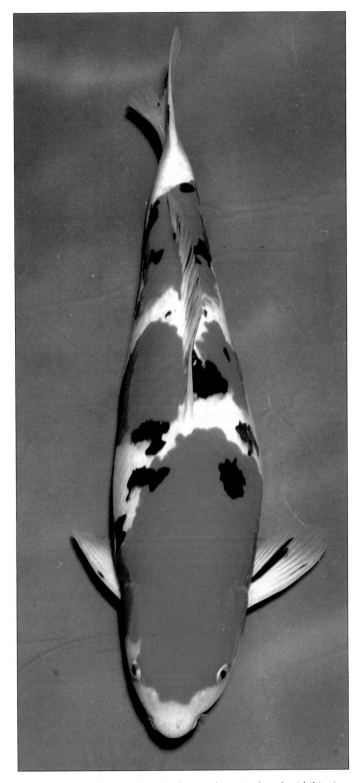

This is a prize-winning Taisho Sanke tri-colored nishikigoi.

A prize-winning Taisho Sanke. This is basically a white fish with red and black markings. Compare it to the Showa Sanke, or the Modern Tri-color on the facing page.

cations for Taisho Sanke vary with each judge. Basically, the black or "Sumi" should not appear on the head forward of the insertion of the pectoral fins. The number of black rays on each paired fin should be limited to a maximum of three. The Japanese have concluded that when there are two or three or even one black marking on the pectoral fin, it means that the color of this particular strain is fixed in this specimen and it could be depended upon to produce good quality offspring. For whatever reason, when Taisho Sanke have lipstick markings and are called "Kuchibeni Taisho Sanke," this is a desirable characteristic whereas the lipstick on the Kohaku is not desirable. The space on the last inch of the body before the tail starts, must be white. If the red and black goes all of the way to the tail, it is a fault and is not appreciated.

Normally black is not supposed to appear on the head, but if the black is particularly balanced or part of a design then it is appreciated. While the pectoral fins are required to have preferably two or three stripes each, the other fins must be perfectly white without any red.

There is a great deal of argument between judges as to whether small blotches of black on the red and white field are more beautiful than large blotches of black. That is just a matter of taste. Of course, as with all kinds of Koi there is the Doitsu variety which in all of the color varieties is normal. Taisho Sanke are available with different scalations. With the Doitsu Sanke the scales should be neatly arranged and not be scattered haphazardly. Very often some of the black spots which are found on young fish enlarge and/or disappear as the fish gets older. Experienced breeders can tell which kind of black spot will be reproduced when the fish is larger and which will disappear.

Unlike the black which may appear in red swordtail tropical fish, there does not seem to be any cancerous melanoma associated with the black which appears in Koi.

SHOWA SANKE

The Showa Sanke is usually referred to by aficionados as "Showa." The term Showa is applied to Emperor Hirohito's era which roughly started in 1924 and is continuing at the time this is written in March, 1988. Basically, the Showa is a three-

lor fish of red, white, and black. If you think of
the Taisho Sanke as a 3-color fish with the same
three colors, you can appreciate that there is a difference between these two 3-color fish. One famous Japanese writer said "Think of starting drawing the same picture on a white canvas and on a
black canvas. On the black canvas, you paint in
the white and the red. On the white canvas, you
paint in the black and red." So basically the difference is the Taisho Sanke is a fish with a predomi-
nantly white background ·with red and black
markings, while Showa Sanke is a fish which is
basically black with white predominating. There
are many other differences.

The Showa Sanke was first produced in the late
1920's by crossing between a Kohaku (red and
white) and Ki Utsuri (black and yellow Koi). During the mid 1960's the yellow-orange which was
characteristic of all of the Kohakus, Taisho Sankes,
and Showa Sankes, became more deeply inbred
until they became as they are at the present, a
deep blood red. Unlike Taisho Sanke, where the
red can be uniform and contiguous, the black in
Showa Sanke must not have a massive pattern.
When viewed from the top the Japanese use the
term "lightning" to define the desired pattern of
the black. Good Showas must have black on the
head as well as red. They also must have a very
important characteristic known as "Motoguro."
Motoguro is the black spot at the base of the pectoral fins. Taisho Sanke must not have this spot.

There are many varieties of Showa, including Hi
Showa (red or orange Showa), which is basically
a red fish; Kage Showa is a fish whose black has
a beautiful net-like appearance; Kindai Showa
which is a modern Showa, is a fish in which the
white predominates and there is little black. Of
course, the Kindai Showa might easily be mis-
taken for a Taisho Sanke, except for the Motoguro,
the black spot, at the base of pectoral fins.

The Showa Sanke must be standardized like
other Nishikigoi fishes. The colors must be intense
and have a clear outline. There should not be
overlaps or shadings. The red must be blood red
and intense, while the white must be pure without
yellow tinges. The black must be as black as possible. "Black as coal" is probably the best kind of
determination. The black pattern should wrap all
around the body, and not just be along the dorsal
edge. Viewed from the top, the Showa's black
must have an interesting pattern. Some people
have blacks which are lightning shape, while
other people visualize maps of different parts of
the world. In any case, the beauty of the observa-

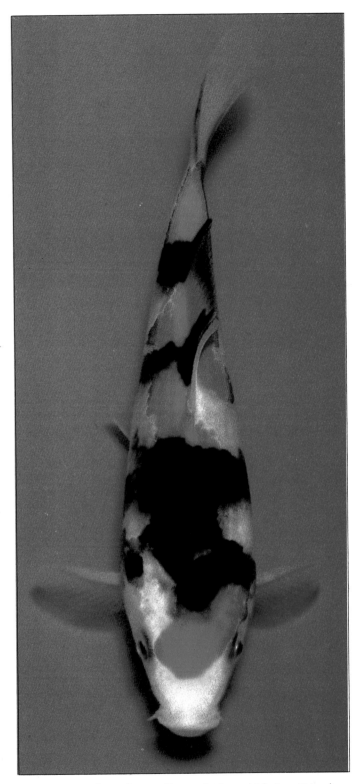

This is a Modern Showa, Showa Sanke, which is a Tri-color
but there is a basically black base upon which red and white
are incidental markings.

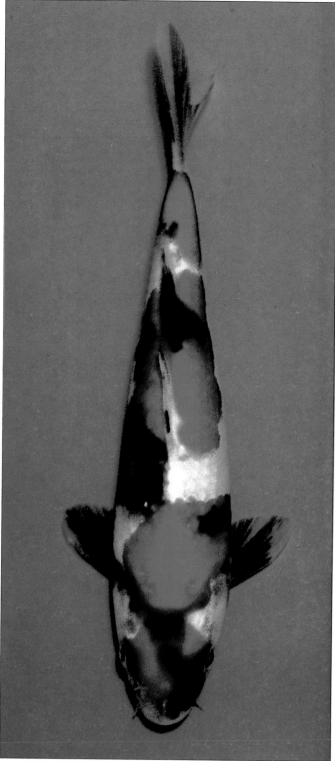

A Prize-winning Showa Sanke.

tion varies from one individual to the other, and certainly from one judge to the next.

The Showa Sanke is one of the three most popular fishes along with Taisho Sanke and Kohaku. It must have the red spot on the head called the Hi. This is, of course, a replica of the Japanese flag. Young Showa Sanke rarely show the intensities of coloration that are desirable in the larger fish. Sometimes a light orange appears. Under proper feeding, the orange becomes an intense red when the fish matures. Whereas with the other three color fish, Taisho Sanko, the pectoral or breast fin may or may not be marked by black, it is absolutely a necessity that Showa Sanke have a black spot on the base of the pectoral fins. These black spots, called Motoguro is explained above, literally translate into "the beginning of black coloration."

Showa Sanke which are mostly red on the back with very little white on the back, are called Hi Showa. "Hi Showa" means "Red Showa."

Boke Showa are three colored fish whose black is mottled or indistinct. "Boke" means "indistinct" or "out of focus."

Kindai Showa are the same three colored fish. "Kindai" means "modern." These are the fish which predominate today. A Kindai Showa is a Showa where white predominates and black is relatively insignificant. Keep in mind though, at all times, the black spot on the base of the pectoral fins called Motoguro, must always be present. Except for these marks it is almost impossible to differentiate between the Taisho Sanke and the Kindai Showa sub-variety of the Showa Sanke. While the black spot on the base of the breast fins is characteristic, Showa Sanke may also have a black mark on the tip of its nose. Its mouth may also have black markings.

There are some Showa Sanke which have no red on the body with the exception of the Hi spot which is the red spot on the top of the head. Such fish are called "Tancho Showa." Tancho is the beautiful red crane. The red crane is symbolic of Japan and it seems only to be found in Japan. Japan Airlines, for example, uses the Tancho Zuru as its symbol. This is an open winged Tancho.

There are varieties of Nishikigoi which are called Tancho. We will discuss these later. But basically they are fish which have the round marking called the Hi spot, which is red and only found on the head. Such a fish is called Tancho which is a grouping including many sub-varieties.

Sometimes Showa Sanke are cross-bred with Ogon Koi. Ogon are metallic gold Koi. Their scales become shiny and they really look like metallic gold when you see them. Such fish are called "Kin Showa" which means "modern golds." The Japanese do not appreciate the metallic appearance of scales. They say this is a German characteristic of the Doitsu. Most English speaking Koi lovers, however, find the metallic appearance of the scales fascinating and they tend to put a lot more value on them than the pale bleached yellow which is to be found in such other varieties as the Asagi.

Thus, a good Kin Showa would be a fish which is the same as the Taisho Sanke or the Showa Sanke where the white is replaced by a golden yellow. If the Motoguro appears, then it is called a Kin Showa. Otherwise, it would be a sub-variety of the Taisho Sanke and would be called a Kin Sanke.

These varieties were very rare in the past, but are showing up with more and more regularity, especially in the Utsuri Mono (black plus another color). This will be discussed later. One of the main problems with Kin Showa is that the red is not intense. This is a variety which will probably take another 20 or 30 years to develop, but it appears on the market now and then and you never know how lucky you might be in breeding them.

The Kin Showa has another problem. Showa Sanke are supposed to be three colored fish. Kin Showa are in fact four colored fish; white, yellow, red, and black. The Japanese give you lengthy philosophical arguments about why the Kin Showa is a three colored fish. However, their arguments are not acceptable to the present author. However, I include them here because the Japanese consider Kin Showa as a tri-color fish.

The Japanese use the word "Sumi" to mean a black ink painting usually on white paper. They call the black mark on the head of Showa Sanke as a typical characteristic of Showa Sanke. The ideal modern Showa Sanke have a Y-shaped mark.

Interestingly enough, at the show held in Japan near Haneda Airport in 1988, I saw several Showa Sanke which did not have the Motoguro black spots on the pectoral fins. They had pure white pectoral fins. Several of these were in the finals to be considered for championship, and I questioned the judges about them. They said that "Showa"

meant "modern," and modern means changing and that this might be a change as the black mark on the pectoral fins get smaller and smaller until it eventually disappears. Again this is a philosophical distinction dealing with the evolution of thinking in the Koi business.

Some authors call Showa Sanke as "Showa Sanshoku."

The Japanese have a peculiarity in their language. The number 3 changes as it applies to different objects. The word three by itself is "san." If you want to go to floor number 3 in a hotel, you would ask the elevator operator to take you to "san kai." "San Shoku" is a three color as it applies to a fish. There are different words of three for round objects such as glasses and bottles; for circular objects such as dishes; etc. There might 20 or 30 different ways to use the number 3 in the Japanese language. This is very confusing to English speaking people who have only 4 or 5 ways to refer to 3 such as three, third, tri, triple, triangular, etc.

The author with two generations of managers of Kamihata. One is an expert on tropical fishes, the other answers questions about koi. At the 1988 All-Japan Nishikigoi Show they were busy the entire two days the show was open solving technical problems for their customers.

COMPETITION CHARACTERISTICS OF A GOOD SHOWA SANKE

As described above, Showa Sanke have much in common with Taisho Sanke and Kohaku. First let's look at the Hi spot which is the red spot on top of the head. The same beautiful Hi spot that is valued in the Kohaku is also a preferred characteristic in the Showa. The larger the head Hi, the better. It may cover the whole head of the fish including the nose and cheeks and lips. However, the pattern should be uniform and deeply colored with a blood red. The edges of the Hi must be clearly separated from the white.

White is also very important. About 25% of the body should be white. Naturally, the white should be snow-white. Some judges would like to see a white area along the back of the fish so that when viewed from above, you can easily see the three colors namely the red, black and white. Or, with the metallic Showas, you should be able to see the four colors. In any case, the characteristic of every Koi should be appreciated from viewing it from the top.

The opercular area, that is the cheeks, should be white, but not necessarily. The reason is that you do not see the cheeks from the top, though more and more people are beginning to appreciate Koi from a side view.

There is a lot to be said for a Sumi mark, that is a deep black mark, to be surrounded by white instead of being trapped by red. Isolated black markings surrounded by white have more value than isolated black markings surrounded by red, or red and white.

The black Sumi marking on the head may run across the head Hi. In any case, it must be an interesting pattern to look at. The Showa Sanke must in every case have a red Hi on the head as well as the black Sumi. The black markings on the body should be of natural shapes. Nature produces lightning, clouds, lakes, and mountains. It is permissible, and even desirable, for the body Sumi to run around the belly. Large, massive Sumi black markings, such as the red found in Kohaku, are desirable but very rare.

Under no circumstances must any of the fins of a good Showa Sanke have any red. They may, however, have black. Some judges will eliminate fish which do not have black marks at the base of their pectoral fins; others will ignore this characteristic. Good Showa Sanke are much more difficult to find than good Kohaku or Taisho Sanke. That is why Kohaku win most of the prizes and Taisho Sanke win the next most. However, when

Two prize-winning Sanke.

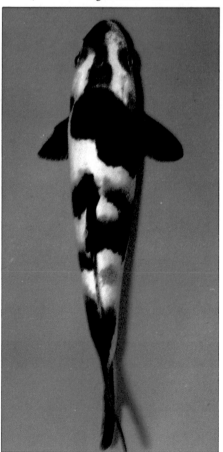

good Showa Sanke shows up, it usually wins ome kind of prize because it is so rare.

ASAGI AND SHUSUI

These are two completely different fishes which, or some unknown reason, are grouped together in very Japanese competition.

"Asagi" means "light blue." It is the earliest lishikigoi known. According to some authorities, rofessor Kichigoro Akiyama, who was a Professor t the National Institute of Fisheries, produced this

An Asagi prize-winning nishikigoi. Asagi means light blue.

This is a much better Asagi than the fish to the left. Not only is the coloration better, but the light edge of each scale is more contrasting.

strain of fish. He said that he produced the Shusui oy breeding a normal German Doitsu mirror carp and with an Asagi Sanke. The Asagi is supposed o be one of the first of the colored carps being a mutant or color variety from the original wild carp called "Magoi." "Shusui" means "autumn water." However, it also is referred to as "German olue" because in all cases the Doitsu or German carp, forms the basis for the Shusui.

This koi pond was located in the rear of the Haneda Airport Hotel where the author resided during the 1988 All-Japan Koi show. The red leaves reminded him of the Shusui (autumn water) koi. The Japanese love the color of autumn leaves in their ponds and they leave them there until they lose their color. When nishikigoi have the same pattern as leaves, the fish may be called Shusui even if they are not really standardized.

Show specimens of Asagi have a beautiful blue coloration when viewed from the top. Each scale is completely surrounded with a white pattern producing a net-like effect upon the fish. Study closely the accompanying photographs and you can easily see what I mean. Now take the same Asagi fish and change the scale pattern to that of the Doitsu and you have a Shusui. This is what Professor Akiyama did in 1904 with fish from Germany forming the basis of the Doitsu lines. The word "Shusui," meaning autumn water, is sup-

Autumn leaves floating artistically in a Japanese koi pond.

posed to conjure up the vision of the reflection of autumn leaves which have turned red, reflecting in the water against the cloudless blue sky. This very relaxing and beautiful to Japanese people and indicates the value they put on "Wah." Wah is a Chinese or Japanese word meaning relaxation and time for contemplation. It is interesting that Mrs. Axelrod, my wife, uses the term "Wah" to me. After dinner I sit down and relax and she says "Don't bother Dr. Axelrod, he is having his Wah"! Mrs. Axelrod studied the Japanese language.

QUALITY STANDARDS FOR ASAGI

In almost all other Koi, solid colors or deep intense colors are required. These colors are either single unique color or patterns produced by these unique isolated or contiguous colors. The Asagi clearly not in this category. The beauty of the Asagi, which means light blue color, is in the netting effect of the blue scales and the lighter blue or white edging to each scale. This applies to viewing the fish from above as do all color varieties of Koi. Many judges think that a clear head with absolutely no color on it except the color white is desirable. I have never seen a beautiful white on the head of an Asagi, but people do talk about them. Most of the heads seem to have skin which is transparent and reflect the bones and tissue underlying the skin. This gives the clear head skin a mottled, dirty appearance.

There are some Asagi which have red on the bottom of their body. For me this is extremely beautiful, though the Japanese do not require any color at all on the bottom part of Asagi. As a matter of fact, if any red on the body is visible from the top the fish is penalized. This does not apply to any of the fins or to the cheeks from the eye and below. The reason the judges give for rejecting Asagi with red markings which are visible from the top is, when the fish grows older, the red tends to move up to the back. Therefore, you do not want to breed from such a fish because you certainly do not want the red to ruin the contrast between the dark blue and white edging of the scales.

If you think of the Koi as boat floating in the water, the ideal dividing line might be the water line mark along the side of the boat.

There are Asagi which have a red head. These are called "Masked Asagi" or, in Japanese, "Asagi Menkaburi." Certain absolutely necessary characteristics of the Asagi are a uniformly colored head. Either spotless, clean unmarked white; spotless unmarked clean light blue; or a solid color, usually red. Spots on any of these patterns eliminate the fish from competition.

Each blue scale along the dorsal edge must be clear and distinct from the next scale being separated by light blue or white. It is absolutely necessary that Asagi have red on the cheeks below the eye, on the belly, and at the base of the fins. This red should be fiery red. The reason I am using the term "fiery" is that the marking should look like the flames on top of a fire and not be neat and uniform. Some fish have completely red pectoral fins. These fish have a special name called "Shusui Bire." Any colors except blue, red, and white are not considered assets. Any red which appears above the lateral line is negative and should not be admitted in shows. When Sumi, black marks, appear along side the red, it is not an acceptable condition. The Japanese like the stomachs of the fish to be snow-white.

The Japanese have names for all of these different Asagi, the most prized of the Asagi is the Asagi Sanke. These have the characteristic netting of scales on the back, they have a beautiful red Hi marking on the head and the sides, and a snow-white stomach. This is a very rare and a very expensive variety of fish.

SHUSUI, THE GERMAN BLUE

Shusui means "autumn water" in Japanese, though it is referred to in the trade as "The German Blue." Shusui are basically Asagi with Doitsu type scalation. The dorsal scales are blue. Show specimens have absolutely perfectly clear blue scales, in very neat rows. Uniformity is the essence of the Shusui and often the term "net-like" is used to describe the pattern. It is not infrequent that metallic scales appear. In some exceptional fish, bright red appears on the nose, both sides of the cheek, the bottom of the fish, and all of the fins. In any case, red on the pelvic fins seems almost to be a requirement, though nobody will confirm it.

KINDS OF SHUSUI

A single row of scales divided by the dorsal fin, being clear blue in color and completely surrounded in white, remind the Japanese of the autumn blue sky with leaves floating on a small reflecting pool. Without this type of scalation, the Shusui does not exist. The scales must be blue. If the scales are black or grey, the fish must be rejected. Spots of red or black which are visible from the top along the dorsal edge or sides, are not acceptable. However, red on the belly is acceptable.

With millions of Koi being produced, it is amazing that a strain of albinos has never appeared!

The head should be a solid color preferably snow-white. However, this is fairly rare, and light blue is more usual. The face and fin bases must have red Hi on them. Whenever Hi appears on any Shusui, it must be fiery red. While additional scales may be found on other parts of the body, the standard applies mainly to the scales which run along the dorsal edge of the fish. They basically must be bilaterally symmetrical. This means what is one side of the dorsal fin must appear on the other side of the dorsal fin.

The Shusui, or German Blue. This is a prize-winning fish.

A beautiful, prize-winning Shusui. These fish can be very effective in competitions and exceptional fish like the one shown here can command very high prices.

Ki Shusui are the same as the Hi Shusui except they have yellow instead of red. For whatever rea son the Ki Shusui are not as dramatic as the H Shusui. I have seen many Hi Shusui and Ki Shusu that have Sumi scales or black scales on the back. Some Koi judges refer to this fish as the "Matsuba Doitsu."

Shusui and Asagi patterns are clearly the bas for many more complex and interesting color pa terns. It is expected that more and more will sho up in the future. At the present time in Japar highly colorful Shusui and Asagi fishes are not ap preciated. The Japanese prefer modest coloratio in these two varieties.

Any randomly scattered scales on the body must be balanced in appearance. Sometimes these scale groups are beautiful, sometimes they are not. It really depends upon the judge. There can be a dozen different kinds of Shusui with Hi Shusui meaning Red Shusui; Hana Shusui meaning Flower Shusui, which are Shusui with red mark- ings on the sides between the dorsal edge and the lateral line.

Ordinarily any red above the lateral line is a negative characteristic, but if the red is really beautiful then the fish is called the "Hana Shusui" and is acceptable.

The Hi Shusui are Nishikigoi which has red all over the back. The Hi must be extremely bright. It is only when this marking makes a fish extremely striking that the judges will accept this extension of the red onto the back.

TANCHO

Tancho is the name of the Japanese cran which has a red spot on its head. Japan Airline uses the Tancho with outspread wings as its syn bol, but color the whole bird red!

Because the Tancho bird is so big and so di tinctive, the same is expected of the fish called th "Tancho." Essentially Tancho Koi first got i name by appearing as a sub-variety or a type c Kohaku. The Kohaku is a two colored fish, bein red and white. So certainly there is a Tancho Kc haku. This is a fish which only has a round re mark on its head with the rest of its body bein white. A lot of credit is given to the fish base upon how perfect is the circle of red, how intens it is, and what is the body shape.

If you study the pictures in this book, you wi see that Koi have basically either round heads c slightly pointed heads. With the Tancho Kohaku broad flat head is desirable so that the round re Hi spot on the head is outstanding. This fish mu: be perfectly formed, have beautiful scales, and re mind the Japanese of their crane.

The reason that the crane, the Tancho, is re vered in Japan is because it also is a symbol of th Japanese flag, the rising sun! Some Japanese refe to this variety, that is an all white fish with just red spot on its head not only as Tancho Kohak but also as "Hinomaru." Hinomaru is the nation; flag of Japan.

Other varieties of Tancho are recognized. The [Be]kko, which is a group of fish which has small [Su]mi or black spots on a uniform base color, may [als]o have the Tancho mark or appearance. Thus, [Ta]ncho with Shiro Bekko are called "Tancho [Be]kke." "Shiro," by the way, refers to white.

[I]n Tancho Sanke, there should not be any black [m]arking on the head. The black markings, or [Su]mi, should be as black as coal and should be [cle]ar, distinct, and interesting. There should be a [fe]w black marks on the pectoral fins to indicate [th]e quality of the genetic lines. Fishes which have [the]se black marks are considered fixed strains.

[In] Tancho Showa, the modern Tancho, must have [a] characteristic round red Hi spot on the head [tog]ether with a body form and color markings of [th]e Shiro Utsuri. Shiro Utsuri are black fishes with [wh]ite markings. Of course, white markings on [bla]ck is also one way to interpret Shiro Utsuri. [Ho]wever, consider a black and white fish with a [re]d Hi and you have the Tancho Sanke. Tancho [Sa]nke is merely a three colored fish the red Hi be-[in]g on the head, the white body and black mark-[ing]s strewn delicately and tastefully around the [bo]dy.

[In] the Tancho Showa, the modern Tancho, I [ha]ve seen at least a dozen magnificent fish where [th]e head black Sumi markings were running [thr]ough the red Hi marking. If the Sumi has almost [a] V-shape, this is acceptable. If it is just what [loo]ks like an accidental black marking, it is re-[jec]ted. In the Kawarimono catch-all group, almost [an]y color variety with a Tancho marking is inter-[est]ing and valuable, though it is not by any means [a v]ery valuable strain unless it is fixed and can be [dup]licated.

[I] have seen many fish which are inverse of the [Ta]ncho Kohaku. If you remember, the Tancho Ko-[ha]ku is a solid white fish with the red round Hi [ma]rking on the head. Can you imagine a fish [wh]ich is all red with a white marking on the head? [Ma]ny of these are to be seen in the Hikari Moyo [cla]ss. No strain has ever been fixed, but some of [the]m are absolutely magnificent, and they do [sho]w up from time to time.

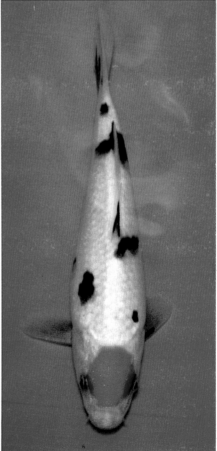

[Th]e two fish shown here are Tanchos. The Tancho is the Jap-[ane]se crane which has a red spot on its head. This red spot [dis]tinguishes it from all other cranes. Usually the red Hi spot [on] the head must be pure, but there are cases when interest-[ing] black markings are acceptable.

UTSURI MONO

Utsuri Mono is a wide ranging group of Nishiki-goi. Basically they are a black fish. The black fish is colored with a second color. The second color can either be yellow, red, or white. Other colors have been appearing now and again, but the strain has not been fixed.

Standards for Utsuri Mono vary considerably. Essentially the fish should be basically black and all of its fins should be prominently marked with black. The more black in the fins, the more attractive is the fish. I recently observed a Utsuri Mono in which the body was golden red and all of the fins were black. There was no black on the body at all. This fish caught everybody's attention, but did not win a prize because it was "too radical a departure from normal."

Ki Utsuri is a black fish with yellow or orange coloring. The yellow or orange coloring must have a lightning pattern or a pattern which is interesting. The black pattern, of course, is the base color so it is not judged, only the yellow pattern. The black must be as black as coal. The yellow or orange color should be uniform and attractive.

Hi Utsuri is red and black. All of the fins m[ust] be prominently marked with black, as in all Uts[uri] Mono, and the red should be as intense and fi[ery] as possible.

The Shiro Utsuri is a black and white fish. Act[u]ally it is white on black where most of the color [is] black. Again, all of the fins must be prominen[tly] marked with black and the whites must be sno[w] white. When there is more white than black, t[he] fish is called a Bekko.

BEKKO

Bekko is a group of Koi whose basic color [is] white, yellow, orange, or red and which has spo[ts,] blotches, or patterns of black. It differs from Uts[uri] because the black marking are much smaller a[nd] more dispersed.

Aka Bekko are black spots basically on a r[ed]

A prize-winning Utsuri Mono. They are black fish with a second color.

A prize-winning Bekko.

h. Shiro Bekko has black spots on a white fish. .ere are many, many other combinations. Basi- lly all of them are defective Sanke fish. If you member, Taisho Sanke and Showa Sanke are ree-colored fish usually white, red, and black. In e Bekko, one of the colors is missing.

It really is true that when Sanke varieties are ed, many Bekko varieties are produced as a by- oduct. When you consider the Bekko varieties d the Utsuri Mono varieties, and you consider eir color combinations and scalations, you can agine how the number of different kinds of Koi ultiplies drastically!

The three fish shown on this page are all prize-winning Bekkos of about the same quality. They took major prizes at the 1987 All-Japan Nishkigoi Show held in Haneda, Japan.

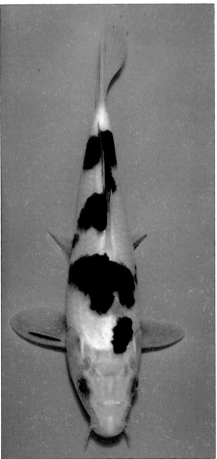

HIKARI UTSURI

Hikari Utsuri are Utsuri, that is two colored fish, except the scales are metallic. In the Utsuri Mono group there are no metallic scales.

In the Bekko group, there are non-metallic base colors involved only.

Therefore, Hikari Utsuri indicates the shiny, golden, or silver varieties of the Utsuri and the Showa. The most popular varieties of Hikari Utsuri are the Kin Ki Utsuri which is a metallic yellow color. This is a lemon yellow and is differentiated from the Kin Showa which is an almost gold metallic fish.

The Kin Shiro Utsuri is a metallic shining silver fish with black natural reflections. Hikari Utsuri were originally bred by crossing Utsuri Mono with Ogon. Ogon refers to the solid metallic gold coloring found in many varieties.

Many of Gin (which means silver), and Kin Shiro (which means silverish black), and Kin Ki (which is metallic yellowish), are derived from the crossing of Utsuri Mono with Ogon.

The silver metallic colors of Kin and Gin Showa comes from crossing Ogon hybrids with Showa Sanke fishes. These are usually known as Kin Showa.

For most beginners in English speaking countries, the metallic fishes are very exciting, very appealing, and attract a lot of attention. Orientals don't think they are exceptional.

This Japanese painting was created during the Edo or Mejii Dynasty during the 1800's. It was painted by Shibata Zeshin who lived from 1807 to 1891. The painting technique was lacquer on paper and may be viewed at the Smithsonian Institution's Freer Gallery of Art. The painting was simply entitled "Carp."

A prize-winning Hikari Utsuri.

On the facing page: Two prize-winn Hikari Utsuri.

HIKARI MUJI

Hikari Muji are single colored Koi which are metallic in appearance. There are many, many names and many, many varieties. Basically, there are the Ogon varieties which are golden in color. The golden color includes the yellow-gold which is called Yamabuki Ogon, and then there is the silver gold Nezu Ogon. One of the most popular varieties is the Matsuba varieties. This variety reminds one of the pine needle. Matsuba in Japanese means "pine needle." Ogon and Hikari Muji are often used for the same fish since "Ogon" means simply "golden." "Hikari refers to "shining" and "Muji" means "self colored" or uni-color.

The Matsuba Ogon and the Kin Matsuba are basically the same fish since Matsuba Ogon can be golden or silver. Ogon means "gold," refers to gold fish in Japanese, but it also includes silver. I suppose the best definition of "Ogon" would be a valuable, heavy metal. Kin Matsuba are golden Matsuba whereas the Gin Matsuba or the Kin Matsuba are silver or platinum metallic colored fish.

A prize-winning Hikari Muji.

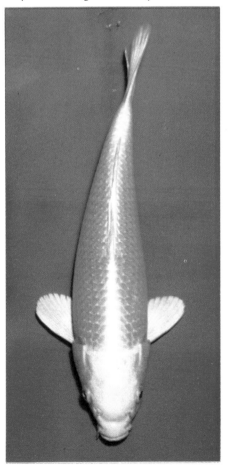

In all cases, the fish of a single color must re[...] win for their general appearance. Their look m[...] be aristocratic and high class. They must have very, very pure color on their head and absolut[...] pure pectoral fins. The metallic body must be v[...] shiny.

There are many other pine needle fishes bes[...] the Matsuba Ogon. There are orange Matsu[...] Ogons, red Matsuba Ogons, and yellow Matsu[...] Ogons. A fiery red Hi Matsuba Ogon is a very r[...] fish. I have heard stories about them, but ha[...] never seen them.

"Gin Matsuba" are often called "Purach[...] Ogon."

HIKARI MOYO

Hikari Moyo are Nishikigoi which have meta[...] and normal color patterns. Hikari means metal[...] and Moyo refers to the patterns. Sometimes the[...] are even additional colors added. Oftentimes th[...]

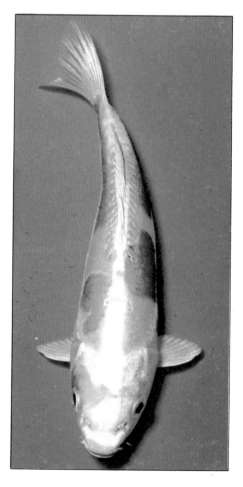

To the left are two prize-winning Hikari Muji. Below is an exceptional Hikari Moyo.

A prize-winning Hikari Moyo.

A prize-winning Hikari Mono.

can be four or five colors. However, basically Hikari Moyo is a general grouping of all fish which have two colorings on them regardless of the other colors, and which don't fit into Hikari, Utsuri, or Hikari Muji groupings. One of the colors must be metallic.

One of the most beautiful of Japanese fishes is referred to as the Kujaku Asagi. The meaning of Kujaku is peacock so that we can expect a metallic varied-color fish, with beautiful metallic marking.

Yamato Nishiki is a metallic Taisho Sanke; Hariwake is a platinum body with yellow patterns; and a Kikusui is the same as a Hariwake but the yellow is tinged with red producing an orange effect. There are many other patterns which are thrown into this Hikari Moyo group. Not all Hikari Moyo fish have only one metallic color. Sometimes Hikari Moyo are fish which have varied color patterns over a metallic base. That is, the whole fish has a metallic coating and the colors on top of it take on the metallic look by itself.

Hikari Mono, on the other hand, are fish which have a basic metallic pattern, but have two or more patterns of other colors. The metallic sheen covers most of the body. The exclusion from this is the Hikari Utsuri, a basically black fish.

KIN AND GIN RIN

The terms "Kin Gin Rin" has many meanings and many interpretations. Basically the three words stand for Kin—gold, Gin—silver color, Rin—scale. Putting them all together you get a golden silver scale, a silver golden scale, or a scale which is golden and silvery or silvery and golden. Take it the way you want it! The idea is that these metallic scales take on a golden appearance when they appear over red and a silvery appearance when they appear over black or white areas. When the scales are spread out looking like metallic deposits or bumps on the fish, the fish is called a Pearl Gin Rin. There are other names applied to it too, but these do not have very great significance.

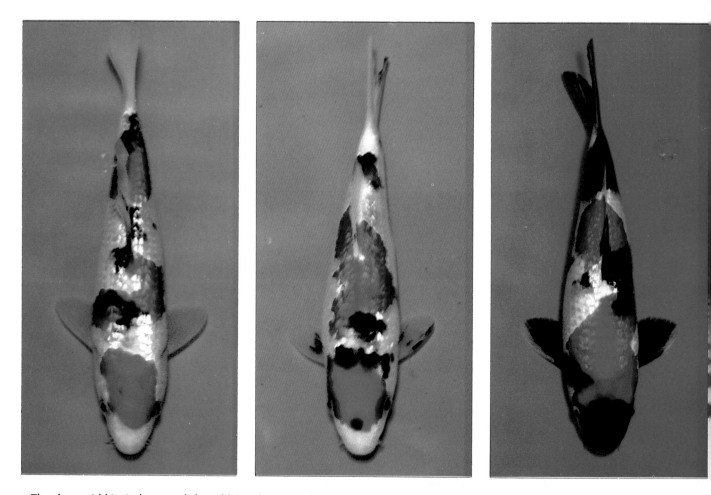

The three nishkigoi above and the additional one on the facing page were prize-winners in the 1987 Haneda All-Japan Nishikigoi Show. They are excellent examples of Kin Gin Rin.

These beautiful Pearl Gin Rin's are especially attractive when they are small, because then the pearls seem large. In looking at the fish, it looks like the scales actually have lumps on them and that you could feel them. You actually can.

Of course, then there is another type of Kin Gin Rin scale which covers the whole body. There are two types of these metallic scales. The first type are the ''Beta-Gin'' where the scale is completely metallicized so that the scale glitters from its entire surface. Really top-quality Kin Gin Rin Nishikigoi are covered with such scales.

Then there are the Diamond Gin Rin, where the scales sparkle from a single point.

Lately there are other types of metallic scales, but all of them seem to be getting mixed up with in-breeding. The Kado Gin is a metallic scale where the sparkling comes from the edge of the scale. ''Kado'' means ''edge'' in Japanese. Some authors refer to them as ''Sudare Gin.'' Sudare are bamboo blinds which cover windows.

Some of these metallic colorings are golden when they cover red, or silver when they cover white or black. Generally speaking, Orientals do not care too much for the metallics because these are ''fools gold'' but they do appreciate beautiful patterns in metallic.

Basically speaking, there is almost an equal number of varieties with metallic scales as without metallic scales. Metallic scale inheritance has nothing much to do with color inheritance. Take for example a typical two colored Kohaku. There is Kin Gin Rin Kohaku which have these metallic golden scales all over the red and where you have silver scales over the white. Should this fish be judged as a Kohaku or should it be judged as a Kin Gin Rin??

The Hiroshima Gin Rin scale is supposed to represent the rays of the sun. The reason that it is called ''Hiroshima Gin Rin'' is because the fish was first discovered in 1969 at the Konishi Koi Farm in Hiroshima. I have never really seen this fish and I do not think anybody else has either. It is best examined by looking at the scales under a microscope and you can see that the scales' ends

KOROMO

Koromo is a Japanese word which means ''robed.''

For the Nishikigoi lover, Koromo are a rare group of Koi which have a silver or blue cast over red and white areas. One of the most exciting of the Koromos is the Aigoromo. The Aigoromo is a Kohaku which is a red and white fish with a bluish cast over the red areas giving the fish an unbelievably majestic look. When the red scales have bluish casts and darker centers, the Kohaku is magnificent. I have seen an Aigoromo change hands on the spot for 10,000 Pounds Sterling which was approximately U.S.$18,000 at the time (1988).

I have also seen magnificent Sumigoromos. You know that Sumi is the name of the black ink that is used in Japan; English speaking people call it India ink. Take a Kohaku which is a red and white fish and put a black robe over the red area and you get a fish that is so magnificent as to defy description. The netting effect on the scales looks more like the petals of a rose or flower than the scales of a fish. It is almost impossible to describe Koromos, so you have to look at the accompanying photographs.

Aigoromos derived their name from the word ''Ai'' which means indigo blue in Japanese. As with all Kohaku, and basically all Koi in general, when red appears it must be a very deep intense Hi red. Hopefully the pattern will be a good Kohaku pattern, and in Aigoromo the area under the robed scales should be dark and absolute blue on the ends. They should be beautifully aligned but the head must be absolutely clear. That is, it should be clear of black scales! If possible, there should be a beautiful Hi on the head. If the Hi on the head has blue edges around it, this is a very unworthy fish in the eyes of the Japanese. When I saw one disqualified in the first round of a competition, I bought it for $100.00. The people around me thought I was crazy to pay so much money for a fish which was only good enough to eat! However, the young boy that I bought it from thought it was just as beautiful as I did. It still swims in my Koi pond in New Jersey.

There are many other types of Koromo. I have seen one fish which instead of having Ai (indigo blue) scales, it had deep, dark Sumi black, scales. This Sumigoromo also had the Sumi markings on the head. This seemed to have been acceptable to the judges at that time, but it was a new interpretation of the standard for me.

The grape robed Koi, the ''Budo Sanke,'' are occasionally a by-product of the Asagi X Kohaku

have a radiation-type effect where each scale has patterns of streaks with red and white in between. This is merely mentioned to indicate how ''beauty lies in the eyes of the beholder.''

Many judges and authors on Koi try to describe very isolated scale and color types or color combination types. These only should be defined when breeding two fish with the same characteristics produce a predictable result. This is, after all, what the breeding of fancy animals is all about. If every time you breed two fish together, you do not know what is going to come out, you might quickly lose interest in selective breeding.

The world of pet animals including dogs, cats, chickens, pigeons, etc., wants to have standards against which they can measure the success of their breeding program. Unfortunately, in some of these exotic Koi, the standards are just inapplicable.

cross. This is the way Aigoromo are produced. It has not, however, become well established enough for standards to be written and accepted.

"Hagoromo" are the same as "Aigoromo" in that they have blue over their red body scales, but the gill plates as well as the pectoral fins are blood red.

There are many, many other types of Koi with these markings and as you can imagine, every color variety can have its own robed appearance. Again there is the constant argument that Koromos are really three-colored fish and they, therefore, should be Sankes!

KAWARIMONO

The final color classification is a Kawarimono. The Kawarimono is the barrel at the end of the rainbow into which everything falls that is not in any of the previous 12 classifications. There are literally thousands of or perhaps evens tens of thousands of different Kawarimono fishes. Some of them are fixed strains already. However, Kawarimono are tending to be isolated and categorized so that the most desirable colors and color patterns can be inbred and perhaps a new variety can be produced.

Dr. Takeo Kuroki produced a beautiful book in which he had many pictures of unique Koi. These are Koi that perhaps only existed in one specimen and which could not be assigned to a specific variety. These are what we would call Kawarimono now. Dr. Kuroki made a very great contribution by publishing some of these photos, but it would take a book with thousands of photos of different varieties to really define the problem. The names attributed to these unique fish are just descriptive terms made up by Dr. Kuroki. Most of the names are taken from the basic names of the first twelve categories of fishes described above, with adjectives trying to describe additional colors or patterns which make them different from the standard types.

By the way, the pronunciation of Japanese is fairly easy for most people of the world because there are no tongue twisting or nasal expressions which are difficult to English speaking people, nor are there sounds produced in the throat, but vowels like i or u are occasionally dropped. Thus "Nishikigoi" is pronounced "Nish-Key-Goy."

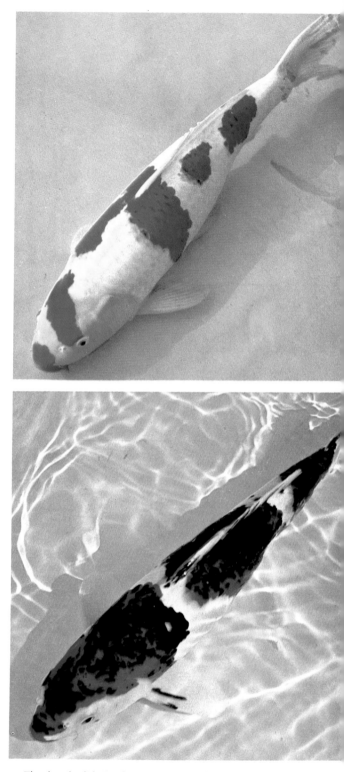

The lovely fish in the uppermost photograph is an Aigoromo.

It is also a Kuchibeni because of the lipstick markings. The lower fish is a nice example of a Sumigoromo, which has a black Sumi marking on top of the red.

The Three-colored koi shown above is an Aigoromo Sanke. Its scales are dark blue and not black (those on top of the red). The other four fishes shown on this page are Kawarimono. Kawarimono are fish which don't fit into any other category.

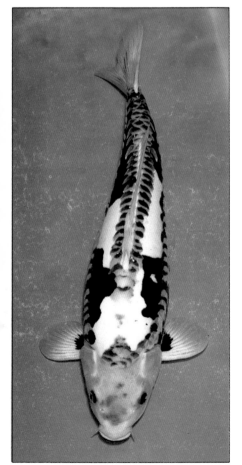

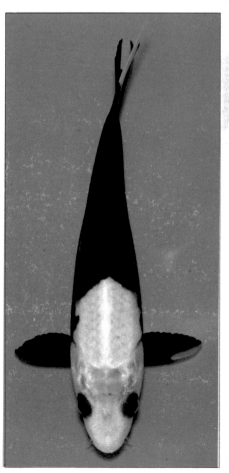

The golden fish uppermost is the famed Kin Matsuba, which is a combination of the metallic Kin (red or combination of yellow/red) and the pine needle or Matsuba. The lower fish is the white Gin Sui together with the Matsuba pattern. This fish is a Gin Matsuba.

KIN OR GIN

The Kin or Gin Sui fish are Nishikigoi which have sparkling metallic lusters. Those metallic fish which have red colorings are called Kin Sui; those that have white coloring are called Gin Sui. Kin Sui by the way means "robed" or "brocaded waters" while Gin Sui refers to "silver waters." Both Kin Sui and Gin Sui are valuable only as young fish. After they get to about two years of age, their colors fade.

KIKU SUI

Kiku sui, which means "chrysanthemum water," is a German-scale Koi which has a metallic sheen to the scale. Often these fish are called Yamabuki which means bright yellow. They also occur in orange-gold, and platinum. This is a very, very rare fish and is seldom seen. However, it does show up on price lists. They are very expensive.

GO SHIKI

The word "Go" in Japanese means five. Go Shiki is five colors. A fish with five colors or with a mixture of colors which is more than five is referred to as a "Go Shiki." Actually, reds and blues which overlap into purples particularly on the head, are called Goshiki. It is a very popular variety with Japanese Koi fanciers, even though standards have not yet been established for it.

MATSUBA

Matsuba means "pine needle." It is a very popular and desirable fish. Many types of Matsuba are available, and there are many more types which take a lot of imagination to appreciate.

Matsuba and Asagi are both related color varieties showing the basic bluish color pattern which fades away to a white belly. If you think about it most fishes have a white belly. Scientists tell us that the reason for this is that when another fish looks at it from below, it can't see the fish because the white blends with the sky. This is true of Koi as well.

It is natural for Koi to have white bellies, thus the Matsuba and the Asagi are two varieties which have a fading color pattern as the scales reach the belly area. The Ki Matsuba, which is a yellow

Prize-winning Kawarimono.

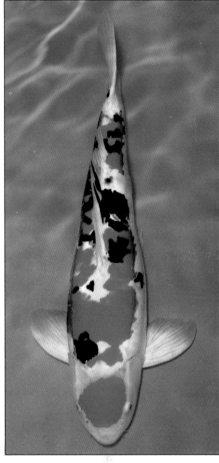

Doitsu prize-winner.

Prize-winning Taisho Sanke.

Prize-winning Showa Utsuri.

Prize-winning Kawarimono.

Matsuba, is supposed to have derived from the Asagi. It is a yellow fish with scales which are grey blue. Really top-quality fish have dark colored blue scales running along the back. The metallic Ki Matsuba is available in brown, red, orange, or yellow, and has each one of the scales tipped in black. These are called "Matsuba Ogon." This means "golden pine needle." Aka Matsuba, the red Matsuba, are like the Ki Matsuba except the basic color of the fish is red.

Japanese price lists for Koi also list several other color varieties even though they are not recognized as pure strains.

YAMATO

Yamato Nishiki which means "Japanese brocade" were very popular at the 1988 Haneda Koi Show. They were produced by crossing a golden Ogon with a Taisho Sanke three-color. Actually it is a psychedelic fish! The ones I saw had a solid red head, with color running from the top all around the bottom. Golden silver scales were shining all over its body and the red was a fiery deep blood red. Oh, what a magnificent fish this was! The fish I saw traded hands for 8,000 Pounds Sterling or approximately US$15,000.

The fish uppermost is the famous Black Crow or Karasugoi. The lower fish is the same Black Crow but it has white pelvics which earn it the name White Wings.

KARASUGOI

The Karasugoi or the "Black Crow" Nishikigoi is just a black single color fish. It really might be better classified as a Hikari Muji (self colored fish), but it is not metallic. When the color of large Karasugoi is intense black and the fish is big, it is a magnificent fish to behold. When the color is grey it is ugly. There are some Karasugoi whose pelvic fins are white. These are called "White Wings." There are also Karasugoi with a white head and these are called "Baldies." And they are even some which have their head, pelvis, and tail which are white. These are called "Yotsujiro," which means four whites.

Sometimes some fish have a white and black marbled appearance. Such fish are referred to often as a "Sumie." A Sumie is a black and white Japanese drawing of a dragon. These fish officially are called Nine Spot Dragons or Kumonryu. Don't confuse "Sumie" with "Sumi" (Black).

REAL AND ARTIFICIAL COLORING IN KOI

uring my 1988 trip to Southeast Asia I discov-
ed that Koi and other fishes were injected with
es to bring out coloring. This is similar to tattoo-
g, except that the fish seem to die after three to
months. However, my experience with the fish
ing was limited to tropical aquarium fishes and
t to the big, strong and hardy carp.

There is, however, a technique in Japan re-
rred to as "Iroage." Iroage means "bringing out
e colors."

The Japanese accept bringing out the colors or
oage, as a technique of getting the fish in best
ndition. They rationalize that if the fish did not
ive the basic color pigmentation, Iroage would
t help. Injecting color is totally rejected!

There are many ways of bringing out the color
fishes. The most dramatic way, of course, is us-
g sex hormones. Inasmuch as the use of sex hor-
ones is dangerous, both to the fish and to the
ople using them, especially when there are
ung children around, we can only warn against
ing hormones. It is not natural to increase the
xual hormone production of a fish for color-
ion, though it is acceptable to use injections of
rtain hormones to aid in reproduction so that ar-
icial reproduction can progress.

The best way to bring out color in fishes is by
ljusting their food and environment. Unfortu-
ately, the most popular brands of food sold in the
glish speaking world are of European or Ameri-
n origin. They do not contain those elements
hich makes Koi colorful. The reason for this is
at the major manufacturers do not experiment
th Goldfish or Koi. The Japanese, especially
mihata who produces a line of Koi food called
Hikari," has spent almost 100 years in producing
od which will make the Koi grow fastest and
ll produce the most color. I single out Kamihata
cause they are also one of the largest producers
colorful Koi and Goldfish. They must feed their
h the food they produce, so you can be sure that
eir food works otherwise their fish would not be
e best there is! I am told, after visiting Kamihata
Japan in 1988, that dried shrimp is extremely
lpful for the production of red pigments. They
so told me about Chlorella which is an alga
alga" is the singular of the more familiar word

Dr. Warren Burgess photographed these Glassfish, *Chanda ranga*, which were injected with coloring. Normally the fish is glass clear without any coloration at all.

Kamihata, the world's largest koi breeder, also is the world's best producer of food for koi and goldfish under the name Hikari.

algae). When you have fish which are pure white, do not feed them anything to bring out the color because the use of Chlorella, for example, will make the fish appear pink. Spirulina is a kind of alga which is grown in Mexico. Many Koi people have found that by using Spirulina they have been able to make the red color a very deep dark red.

Water quality is also important for the health of the fish. You cannot expect a fish to be in good color if it is sick or fighting for its life in filthy water. Koi can take a lot of abuse. They are a very strong fish, and they can live under conditions that most other fish cannot live under, but there is a limit! They are especially sensitive to lack of dissolved oxygen in the water.

A Chinese carp pond in Hong Kong at the Hong Kong Aquarium. Unfortunately the water is so dirty that the koi are only visible when they come up for the floating pellets which are offered by visitors. Photo by Dr. Arthur Topilow.

This koi pond is just starting to fill with water. The banks have been formed of large rocks which are cemented together. The plants have been located where they will look natural when the pond is filled with water. Photo by Dr. Arthur Topilow.

his was once swampy marshland. The swamp was drained by digging out parts of it and putting the dredge on the banks to
orm an informal series of ponds. The large trees were preserved in an island environment. A pond this large is impossible to
eep clean and only floating pellets bring the nishikigoi into sight.

is springtime, which means cherry-blossom time in Tokyo, Japan. This is a favored time of the year. The cherry blossoms fall
nto the top of the koi pond giving the imaginative Japanese yet another dimension to the beauty of their pond. Cherry blossom,
r Sakura in Japanese, is also the name of a koi. When there are no cherry blossoms left to fall onto the pond, colored koi remind
1em of these lovely times. Those koi which have cherry blossom designs are called Goten-zakura nishikigoi.

5. DOITSU, THE GERMAN CARP

In the 17th Century, European paintings depict what is generally considered to be carp-like fishes with defective or deficient scalation. These fishes were inbred in an attempt to breed a fish completely without scales, thus saving the cook the chore of removing the scales. Hundreds of years later this German carp, as it was called, found its way into Japan. The Japanese called this fish "doitsu". Doitsu in Japanese means "German".

In the early 20th Century, Japanese koi breeders began experimenting with the German carp, Doitsu, because the Doitsu had a heavier body and seemed more hardy than the Japanese carp. The wild carp had already been bred in China and Japan, but these had normal scales, even though the wild color had already been displaced by white and red fish.

The Japanese hardly paid attention to the in

Kinsui or Kin Shusui is a lovely Doitsu or German carp which has been bred to exhibit the characteristics of the Striped Carp with dorsal and lateral line scales, plus the metallic scales and even the lipstick, Kuchibeni.

eritance of scalation because they knew that the heritance of color in koi was unpredictable. Little did they know that scale pattern was more Mendelian (predictable) and with a little bit of knowledge they could do very well with guessing what type of offspring defectively scaled carp, the Doitsu are just that, would produce.

There are five basic scalations to be found on German carp. These German carp differ from the wild carps of Japan, the Magoi, by their height to length ratio. The German carps are much heavier, thus their height to length ratio is smaller than that found in Magoi, the Japanese wild carps.

The five types of scales are:

1. The fully scaled fish wherein the fish is covered with scales.

2. Fish where the scales essentially are found only on the back, almost symmetrical on both sides of the dorsal fin. These fish are called Mirror carp.

3. Fish where the scales are found along the back as in the Mirror carp, as well as along the lateral line. These may be referred to as "Striped" carps.

4. Fish where there are no scales at all are called "Leather" carp.

5. Fish which have random exaggerated scales strewn about their bodies; these are still referred to as "German" carp.

The uppermost fish is a Peacock Gold or Kujaku Ogon with a Striped Koi pattern. The lower fish is also a Striped German Carp which the Japanese call Kiku Sui.

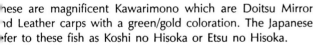

These are magnificent Kawarimono which are Doitsu Mirror and Leather carps with a green/gold coloration. The Japanese refer to these fish as Koshi no Hisoka or Etsu no Hisoka.

THE INHERITANCE OF SCALATION

The inheritance of scalation is controlled by two genes, associated with their mutants or alleles. The gene **S** we shall use to designate SCALED FISH. Its allele, **s,** will be used to designate the mutant gene which stops the formation of scales. Every normal fish must have an **S** gene, but they can also have either another normal **S** gene or an abnormal **s** gene. Fish which have two of the same genes for a single characteristic are called HOMOZYGOUS. Fish with two different genes are called HETEROZYGOUS. Homozygous fish usually always look either normal or abnormal depending upon which genes they carry. Heterozygous fish look normal but may have an abnormal gene.

The second factor controlling scales is the factor **N** which stands for NO SCALES. We use the letter **n** to designate the allele which is a mutant gene meaning scaled. Thus an **nn** fish is normal while an **NN** or **Nn** fish would have abnormal scales. **NN** fish never live. The **SS** fish is normally scaled as is the **Ss,** but the **ss** fish would be abnormal.

Thus we talk about GENOTYPE and PHENOTYPE. The genotype of a fish is what genes it has; the phenotype is what it looks like. We must always be concerned with both of these genetic characteristics in order to selectively breed Koi with special scalation.

When a male and female fish breed, a sin sperm from the male unites with a single egg produce a single offspring. As with all things nature, there are rare exceptions. These rare ceptions produce Siamese twins, fraternal tw and/or identical twins in humans. There are equ alent random fertilizations in fishes, too.

The single sperm and the single egg carry ger for many characteristics. When the sperm and e combine, the male's gene for **S** or **s** combines w the female's gene for **S** or **s;** the same is true the other gene controlling scaleless condition, t **N** or **n** gene. Using a handy little table called Punnett square, we can show the POSSIBILITIES genetic combinations based upon PRESUMED netic makeups of the parents based upon wh they look like. It is only normal-looking fish whi are difficult to determine genetically but by breeding two normal fish and then inbreedi their offspring, a skilled geneticist can usually c termine the genetic makeup, the genotype, of t original breeders.

Our situation here is different. We can see t phenotype, thus we have some idea of the gen type. Probable genetic formulae for the differe Doitsu are as follows:

NORMALLY SCALED KOI: they are either h mozygotic **SSnn** or heterozygotic, **Ssnn.** No oth

German Striped Carp which show the characteristic wild coloration and the scales along the lateral line. These fish have scales along the dorsal edge, too, but they are not visible in this photograph. Photo by Barry Pengilley.

...netic combination can produce a fully scaled ...rp. **SSnn** individuals when bred together can ...ver produce anything but fully scaled individu...— unless there is a genetic accident (mutation). ...u shouldn't count on anything like this happen...g. Using the Punnett square technique, we can ...ualize what the possibilities are. The male ...erm can release either an **S** or an **s** together with ...normal **n** gene. Thus breeding two individuals ...gether, we have the possibility or breeding ei...er two **SSnn's**, two **Ssnn's** or one of each, an ...nn and a **SSnn**. The Punnett square analyses ...own below help you to visualize and predict the ...ssible offspring and the mathematical probabil...of getting a particular kind of offspring.

♀ \ ♂	Sn	Sn	Sn	Sn
Sn	SSnn	SSnn	SSnn	SSnn
Sn	SSnn	SSnn	SSnn	SSnn
Sn	SSnn	SSnn	SSnn	SSnn
Sn	SSnn	SSnn	SSnn	SSnn

CROSSING TWO NORMALLY SCALED KOI WITH TWO HOMOZYGOUS FORMULAE SUCH AS **SSnn × SSnn**. Using the technique of analyzing a Punnett square, we find that 100% of the carp in such a cross are normally scaled and purebred for normal scalation. *Bear in mind that in this case we can expect 100% predictability, but in the cases where more than one kind of offspring are produced, the expected result is merely a probability and not a mathematical certainty.*

...OSSING TWO NORMALLY SCALED CARP. ONE POSSI...ITY IS A HOMOZYGOUS **SSnn**; THE OTHER POSSIBIL...Y IS A HETEROZYGOUS **Ssnn**. There are three possible ...eeding pairs: **SSnn × Ssnn** . . . or **SSnn × SSnn** . . . or **Ssnn** ...Ssnn. The Punnett square analyses follow:

♀ \ ♂	Sn	Sn	sn	sn
Sn	SSnn	SSnn	Ssnn	Ssnn
Sn	SSnn	SSnn	Ssnn	Ssnn
Sn	SSnn	SSnn	Ssnn	Ssnn
Sn	SSnn	SSnn	Ssnn	Ssnn

♀ \ ♂	Sn	Sn	sn	sn
Sn	SSnn	SSnn	Ssnn	Ssnn
Sn	SSnn	SSnn	Ssnn	Ssnn
sn	Ssnn	Ssnn	ssnn	ssnn
sn	Ssnn	Ssnn	ssnn	ssnn

...ROSSING TWO NORMALLY SCALED KOI WITH TWO ...FFERENT GENETIC FORMULAE SUCH AS **SSnn × Ssnn**. ...sing the technique of analyzing a Punnett square, as shown ...ove, we find the following:
...out of 16 or 50% are phenotypically normal with a genetic ...rmula of **Ssnn**;
...out of 16 or 50% have the normally scaled appearance and ...ey are purebred for scalation with the gene formula of **SSnn**.

CROSSING TWO NORMALLY SCALED KOI WITH HETEROZYGOUS GENE FORMULAE SUCH AS **Ssnn × Ssnn**. Using the technique of the Punnett square above, we can expect the probability ratio of:
25% (4 out of 16) **SSnn**. These are homozygous, normally scaled koi;
50% (8 out of 16) **Ssnn**. These are heterozygous, normally scaled koi;
25% (4 out of 16) **ssnn**. These are homozygous Mirror koi or carp.

...his Autumn Sky variety is a Gin Sui or ...ilver Shusui. It is also a German ...Doitsu) Striped Carp.

This yellow carp is called a Kawagoi or Leather Carp (scaleless).

LEATHER OR NAKED, SCALELESS KOI: they are heterozygotic, **ssNn.** Because they must have one **Nn** gene, these fish can never be produced directly from normally scaled koi because normally scaled koi do NOT have an **N** gene but only **n** genes. Remember that only the sperm and egg (germ plasm) carry single gene characteristics. Once fertilization takes place, the body cells carry the genetic combination or two characteristics, one from each parent. Thus an **SS** gene is a body cell which is split into 2 **S** genes when it is carried in an egg or sperm. By using the Punnett square technique, we can predict exactly what possibilities there are by breeding two Leather carps, **ssNn,** together. We could never expect normal fish from such a breeding.

Using a normal looking koi, we can bree them with a Leather koi and test the gene makeup with the following Punnett squa analysis:

♀ \ ♂	sN	sN	sn	sn
Sn	SsNn	SsNn	Ssnn	Ssnn
Sn	SsNn	SsNn	Ssnn	Ssnn
Sn	SsNn	SsNn	Ssnn	Ssnn
Sn	SsNn	SsNn	Ssnn	Ssnn

CROSSING A LEATHER CARP, **ssNn**, WITH A NORMAl SCALED CARP, **SSnn**. This crossing does not produce Leather carp, much to the surprise and dismay of inexp enced koi breeders:
50% (8 out of 16) are Striped koi, **SsNn**, with a line of sc along the lateral line and atop the back;
50% (8 out of 16) are **Ssnn**, which are normally scaled ko

♀ \ ♂	sN	sn	sN	sn
sN	ssNN	ssNn	ssNN	ssNn
sn	ssNn	ssnn	ssNn	ssnn
sN	ssNN	ssNn	ssNN	ssNn
sn	ssNn	ssnn	ssNn	ssnn

CROSSING TWO HETEROZYGOTIC LEATHER CARPS, **ssNn × ssNn.** Using the technique of the Punnett square shown above, we are probably going to get:
25% (4 out of 16) **ssNN**. These fish contain a *lethal gene combination*. The **NN** gene combination results in the embryo dying early in its development, usually before the egg hatches. This often explains why certain pairs of fish produce less than others, even though visually (phenotypically) the fish all look the same:
25% (4 out of 16) **ssnn**. These are homozygous Mirror carp;
50% (8 out of 16) **ssNn**. These are heterozygous Leather carp.

As you can see from these analyses there many, many possibilities. If we further cross offspring of this crossing, more and more possib ties arise. This is a simple example of how y can make genetics work for you.

There is a book, by the way, on fish genet *Genetics For Aquarists* by D. J. Schroder (T 656; 1976) for those who want to learn m about the scientific way to breed fishes. This is excellent book especially written for aquaris Other specialist books published by TFH Public tions, such as their book *All about Bettas, Swo tails, Platies*, etc., contain excellent chapters fish genetics as they apply to those special fish Your local petshop usually stocks TFH books.

♀ \ ♂	Sn	Sn	sn	sn
sN	SsNn	SsNn	ssNn	ssNn
sN	SsNn	SsNn	ssNn	ssNn
sn	Ssnn	Ssnn	ssnn	ssnn
sn	Ssnn	Ssnn	ssnn	ssnn

CROSSING A LEATHER CARP, **ssNn**, WITH A SCALED CARP, **Ssnn**. Utilizing Punnett square analysis and appreciating that this is merely a probability technique, we can expect the following:
25% (4 out of 16) **Ssnn**, normally scaled carp;
25% (4 out of 16) **SsNn**, Striped carp;
25% (4 out of 16) **ssNn**, Leather carp;
25% (4 out of 16) **ssnn**, Mirror carp.
I have used the terms *koi* and *carp* interchangeably. Some people might argue about it, but all koi are carp, but not all carp are koi (unless you are Japanese).

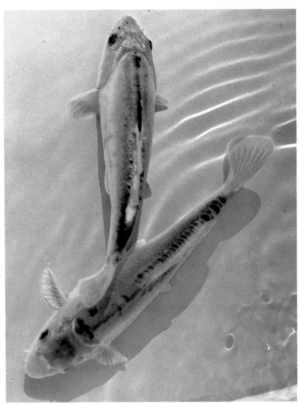

These Mirror Carp are also known as Kinsui.

Yambuki Hariwake is a Striped Carp.

The Orange Hariwake is also a Striped Carp.

MIRROR CARP: these are fishes which have scales along the dorsal edge of the body, usually on both sides of the dorsal fin, fairly symmetrical bilaterally. They are homozygous and must have

(Doitsu) Striped Carp.

only **ssnn** genes. Capital letters, by the way usually designate the dominant gene; recessive genes are designated with small letters. Recessive characteristics are visual only on individuals which are pure (genetically) in recessive genes. This is the case with the Mirror carp and its **ssnn** genetic makeup.

Breeding Mirror carp together can ONLY produce Mirror carp (barring genetic accidents). This is easily seen by using the Punnett square as follows:

♀ \ ♂	sn	sn	sn	sn
sn	ssnn	ssnn	ssnn	ssnn
sn	ssnn	ssnn	ssnn	ssnn
sn	ssnn	ssnn	ssnn	ssnn
sn	ssnn	ssnn	ssnn	ssnn

CROSSING TWO MIRROR CARP, **ssnn × ssnn**. Utilizing our Punnett square techniques we are able to predict the probability of achieving the following results:
100% of the offspring would be Mirror carps.

STRIPED CARP: these are fishes which have both the scalation of the Mirror Carp plus additional rows of scales along the lateral line on both sides of their bodies. The genetic formula for Striped Carp is either **SSNn**, which is heterozy-

gous, or, **SsNn,** which is also heterozygous. Thus, by crossing two of these heterozygous fish together, you can get a very interesting mix because should you happen to select (by chance) **SsNn** fish, you might get EVERY variety of scalation possible, as you can see from the Punnett square below:

♀ \ ♂	SN	Sn	sN	sn
SN	SSNN	SSNn	SsNN	SsNn
Sn	SSNn	SSnn	SsNn	Ssnn
sN	SsNN	SsNn	ssNN	ssNn
sn	SsNn	Ssnn	ssNn	ssnn

CROSSING TWO STRIPED CARP OF THE SAME GENETIC MAKEUP, **SsNn × SsNn**. Crossing two fish which look very similar, such as crossing two Striped carp with the genetic formula of **SsNn**, can produce some surprises, as follows:
4 out of 16, or 25%, will probably never hatch because they contain the **NN** lethal gene combination;
2 out of 16 will be Striped carp with the gene formula **SSNn**;
4 out of 16, 25%, will be Striped carp but their formula will be **SsNn**;
1 out of 16 can be expected to be a normally scaled carp with the genetic formula **SSnn**;
2 out of 16 will be normal with the genetic formula **Ssnn**;
2 out of 16 will be Leather carps with the genetic formula **ssNn**;
1 out of 16 will be the Mirror carp with the genetic formula **ssnn**.

This Yoroi Doitsu is also called the Armored Carp. Actually it is a German carp without purified genetic inheritance. It might well have an **SsNN** gene pattern which is normally lethal.

But you might just as easily have selected an **SSNn** and crossed it with an **SsNn.** Then you would get:

♀＼♂	SN	Sn	SN	Sn
SN	SSNN	SSNn	SSNN	SSNn
Sn	SSNn	SSnn	SSNn	SSnn
sN	SsNN	SsNn	SsNN	SsNn
sn	SsNn	Ssnn	SsNn	Ssnn

CROSSING A STRIPED CARP, **SsNn**, WITH ANOTHER STRIPED CARP, **SSNn**, BOTH HETEROZYGOUS, BUT WITH DIFFERENT GENETIC COMBINATIONS. Although the previous examples could easily be calculated mentally, as the gene combinations become more and more complex, the Punnett square analysis becomes more valuable for the beginning fish geneticist. The crossing, as indicated in the Punnett square above, would be expected to produce:
25% or 4 out of 16 lethal gene combinations. Two each of 16 would be **SSNN** and **SsNN**. The **NN** is a lethal combination for carp;
25% would be **SSNn** Striped carp;
25% would be **SsNn** Striped carp;
25% would be normally scaled carp; 2 of the 4 would have **SSnn** homozygous genes while the other two would be heterozygotic, **Ssnn**.

It probably won't be too long before genetic engineers begin experimenting with nishikigoi. These engineered genetic recombinations might not follow the Mendelian inheritance laws which apply to fishes. Not all fishes have the same number of chromosomes, by the way. Humans have 23 pairs of chromosomes; so do Guppies.

Or, since they all look alike, you might have selected an **SSNn** and crossed it with another **SSNn**. The predictable results would be:

Normally scaled Orange Ogon.

A silver/gold Mirror Doitsu also known as a Kagamigoi.

♀＼♂	SN	SN	Sn	Sn
SN	SSNN	SSNN	SSNn	SSNn
SN	SSNN	SSNN	SSNn	SSNn
Sn	SSNn	SSNn	SSnn	SSnn
Sn	SSNn	SSNn	SSnn	SSnn

CROSSING TWO IDENTICAL STRIPED CARPS, **SSNn** × **SSNn**. From this cross you can expect your Punnett square analysis to indicate the following probabilities:
25% will die because they have the lethal gene combination **NN**;
50%, or 8 out of 16, will be Striped carp because they have the **SSNn** gene formula;
25%, or 4 out of 16, will have the genetic formula **SSnn**, which makes them homozygous normally scaled carp.

GERMAN CARP: these are fish which have random scalation, without pattern and without genetic regularity and predictable breeding results. The reason is that Doitsu are, by definition, genetically defective fish. This defect shows up not only on the scales, but many other ways as well. In terms of finnage, the dorsal fin of most German carps is defective. In terms of producing healthy offspring, as many as 25% of the eggs never hatch, or the hatchling dies immediately after hatching. Grotesque shapes and forms develop in the embryo, most of which are fatal while the embryo is still in the egg. The German carp with random scales, then, is the BEST of this diminutive, genetically defective group. They are the genetically mixed up German carp which have survived the mathematical probabilities of random genetic makeup which allowed them to survive. From a strictly genetic point of view, they are best destroyed, for they can never be stabilized.

Ken Lucas photographed this beautiful koi at the Steinhart Aquarium in San Francisco, California.

Small German carp available in Europe. These are a new breed which have not been introduced to the Oriental market and thus have not been bred with nishikigoi. The normal Striped pattern with the scales along the lateral line has been replaced with a row of scales along the lower edge of the fish. Photographed by B. Walker in 1972.

5. KEEPING KOI

Koi are very hardy fish and they adapt to just about every environment that is neither polluted, poisoned, nor constantly frozen or overheated!

This covers all of the situations which are negative. When you have normal outside garden pools, normal ponds which occur on your own property, or large aquariums for inside the house, the same negative aspects should be avoided. The temperatures should be kept as close to living room temperature as possible. Ideal temperatures are probably between 50° and 75°F for Koi, though my Koi ponds in New Jersey are frozen in the winter and perhaps reach 85° or 90° in the summer. In the winter I do nothing but ensure that the ponds, which are four feet deep at their deepest, do not freeze solid (which they never do).

During the summer when the water gets warm I run a constant flow of spray water. I wanted to take the water from my roof and change the water in the pond every time it rains, but I found that the pollution settling on my roof and the acid rain were detrimental.

Many books advise taking care that the water being used in the Koi pond is free of chemicals. I have never had trouble with using water right from the tap providing I changed 10% or less over a 24 hour period.

This book is not a complete book about how to start with Koi. Basically, it is a book about Koi varieties. I have written several other books which are suitable for starting a Koi pond. You can find these books, and other books at your petshop.

The koi pond originally under the house was allowed to dry out so the floor of the house could be repaired. Small koi ponds are located in various parts of the estate. Isolated ponds are used for spawning. After the eggs are laid, the breeders are once again placed in the large pond under the house, and the fry are raised in the small ponds. When they are about an inch long (2.54 cm), they are sorted and sold.

The koi pond in this lovely Japanese garden is secondary to the gazebo in the center. The hidden filter and pumps activate mini-series of waterfalls which aerate and cleanse the water.

Japanese gardens are created with overgrown luxury or elegant simplicity. This type of garden, with its large koi pond, can easily be duplicated almost anywhere in the world because the shrubbery is temperate and not tropical.

This temple in Japan solved the problem of stray animals, unwelcome guests and mowing the lawn by surrounding itself with a large lake. This is actually an informal moat but the koi in the water, the artistic clump of rocks and stones, and the tastefully located flowering bushes make this a work of art.

The koi ponds are very small and hidden from general view, but as you walk through this lovely Japanese garden, you come across numerous small ponds each containing but a few very colorful koi.

Scenes from a koi pond in Hawaii. Photo by Dr. Arthur Topilow.

This lovely koi pond is in Japan, but it might just have well been located in England or New Jersey. It features hardy water lilies and lovely irises. The cut-down Japanese maples and other small shrubs are easy to grow and maintain.

me koi ponds which are open to the public earn quite a bit
money selling koi food for visitors to feed to the fish.

is very difficult to keep the water in large koi ponds clear
ough for the fish to be visible at all times. With large ponds
e this one, the filtering bed may be as large as the pond (in
rface area).

Photo by Dr. Arthur Topilow.

nall koi stream running alongside the path uses large sitting stones as a walkway guide. By leaning over while seated, the
server can appreciate the nishikigoi at close range. This is a beautiful Japanese garden setting.

In order to protect the plants from being eaten by the koi, mesh fence is put around them. This mesh fence has sever other functions as well. By constantly chewing up the sar and dirt in which most water lilies are planted, the water b comes murky and the filters become clogged. Baby fish ca slip through the holes in the mesh and hide from larger fishe or even be fed separately. Photos by Dr. Arthur Topilow.

The screened-in fenced area is also useful to separate mal from females, or one variety from another. It may also hou breeders and protect their eggs from being eaten by the pond-mates. Photos by Dr. Arthur Topilow.

This informal pond was enhanced by placing large stones around it. It is located in the mountains around Tokyo. A small stream has been diverted to gently replenish the water in the koi pond and keep it fresh and clear. Keeping the water in a koi pond clear is the major problem faced by aquarists. Photo by Dr. Arthur Topilow.

This magnificent Japanese garden utilizes sand designs in the center of which is a very tiny nishikigoi pond made of plastic sheeting. It is wonderful because every time it rains, the sand must be redesigned. This is quite a challenge. It is the author's favorite design.

The best place to keep Koi is in ponds or pools outside your home. The accompanying photographs give you some idea of magnificent pools and ponds in which Koi are successfully kept. The major problem with most pools and ponds which are outside is filtering the water to keep it crystal clear. This is usually a fairly unique filtering job, which requires a lot of engineering skills. Again, without being too apologetic, you are referred to the books listed in the Bibliography in order to get further information about Koi Construction, Garden Ponds, etc.

This moat keeps away unwanted visitors. It is about one meter (40 inches) wide and 30 cm (12 inches) deep. It is lined with heavy plastic and heavy stones have been cemented in place to form a natural looking bank. A small bridge connects the home side of the moat with the opposite bank. The bridge, besides being used for crossing the moat, also serves as an observation deck for watching the koi. Photo by Dr. Arthur Topilow.

This moat can be further decorated by adding plants, such as the papyrus shown here, planted in flowerpots. The pots may be removed in the winter, if necessary. Flowering plants, like tulips, can also be added along the sides of the moat in pots which are not submerged.

KOI SHOWS

There are Koi Shows and Koi Societies found all over the world. You are best advised to contact your local petshop from whom you bought your Koi and ask them to put you in touch with the Koi Society or to advise you about Koi Shows. Once you get involved with Society members, you will find a great fraternity of people who have mutual interests. You will also have the opportunity of discussing local water conditions, the value of fishes, exchange rates, and the other social aspects of any club.

Scenes from the 1988 All-Japan Nishikigoi Show held in Haneda, Japan in January, 1988. The people, above, are members of the Kamihata team. They had a stand at the show. The trophies in the lower photo were part of hundreds of trophies given out in the 169 categories (with three prizes in each category). There are 13 size categories and 13 variety categories; there is a first, second and third prize. There is also a first, second and third BEST IN SHOW PRIZE.

日本配合飼料株

Views inside the All-Japan Nishikigoi Show held in Haneda, Japan, January, 1988. It is estimated that 15,000 nishikigoi were entered in the competition.

The Kamihata stand at the 1988 All-Japan Nishikigoi Show held in Japan, in January, 1988. In the lower photograph, a rather complicated filtering system is being set up to show koi-lovers how to keep their ponds clear. Keeping pond water clear is the major problem facing outdoor aquarists.

7. LONG-FINNED AND PYGMY KOI

s far as Japanese nishikigoi breeders are concerned, the bigger, the better. Thus when koi with long fins appeared in Singapore, the Japanese took little notice. In the All-Japan Nishikigoi Shows held in Haneda for the last few years (1985-1988), not a single long-finned nishikigoi was entered. When I asked the officials about this, they said they didn't know anything about long-finned koi.

I have bred long-finned koi since 1985, having received some fish from my local koi supplier, Murray Wiener of Tropiquarium Petshop in Monmouth County, New Jersey. They were not pretty fish at all, being mostly wild grey. After some inbreeding, I noticed yellows, golds and finally some red and black appearing amongst isolated individuals.

During the spring of 1986, Mr. Wiener received from Singapore a lovely pair of long-fins, about 68 cm long (that's about 25 inches). I put them into my pond to fatten them up. Suddenly three extremely warm days in a row produced a toxic condition in my pond and the two breeders died from a toxic algae bloom which depleted the pond of oxygen. I had nothing else in the pond so I emptied it and refilled it with cold water right from the tap. It took a few days to empty and refill. Imagine my surprise when I discovered hundreds of koi fry swimming around in the cold water. The chlorine and fluorine in New Jersey water didn't seem to bother them. The eggs must have been attached to the plants in the pond. I took some of the fry and used them for an experiment in koi feeding. I was measuring the difference between Japanese koi food and German flake foods.

Within three months there was no question that the Japanese koi food put three times the amount of growth on the koi, so I stopped the experiment and put the experimental animals back into the koi pond, except for a dozen I had difficulty in capturing when my net disappeared. As time went on, the dozen koi hardly grew at all! It now two years since this experiment took place and I have dozens of very long-finned koi in several color varieties. The largest of them is less than 15 cm (6 inches). I have not tried to breed these koi as I wanted to observe them in my large koi aquaria.

But I did further experimentation with feeding koi. If you want to stunt the growth and to have dwarf koi, just put them into an aquarium when they are very small and feed them very limited amounts of flake food. Don't use foods which have more than 35% protein. Feed them as much as they will eat in one minute—but only twice a week. This should produce colorful, stunted koi not larger than 6 inches (15 cm). They seem never to grow larger.

The author, Dr. Herbert R. Axelrod, produced these Long-finned Pygmy Koi. The largest one shown below is 2 years of age and is less than 10 cm in total length.

THE WINNING FISHES IN THE 19TH ALL-JAPAN NISHIKIGOI COMPETITION (1987)

The author wishes to express his thanks to The All-Japan Nishikigoi Promotion Association for their assistance in presenting the winners of their show to English-speaking peoples of the world. Arrangements have already been made to present photographs of future winners in forthcoming editions of this book.

SIZES

The Japanese breeders (farmers) who sponsor the largest nishikigoi show in Japan have had changing size categories. They initially agreed to a 13 size-category system, but as better koi feeds and conditions developed, larger and larger fish were entered in the show and the 19th Annual Show showed the necessity to increase the size categories to include fishes over 80 cm in size (80 cm equals more than 31 inches!). Thus categories 14 and 15 were included. The categories change every 5 cm (2 inches).

Size 1 fish to 15 cm (6 inches)

Size 2 fish to 20 cm (8 inches)

Size 3 fish to 25 cm (10 inches)

Size 4 fish to 30 cm (12 inches)

Size 5 fish to 35 cm (14 inches)

Size 6 fish to 40 cm (16 inches)

Size 7 fish to 45 cm (18 inches)

Size 8 fish to 50 cm (20 inches)

Size 9 fish to 55 cm (22 inches)

Size 10 fish to 60 cm (24 inches)

Size 11 fish to 65 cm (26 inches)

Size 12 fish to 70 cm (28 inches)

Size 13 fish to 75 cm (30 inches)

Size 14 fish to 80 cm (32 inches)

Size 15 fish anything larger than 80 cm

出品鯉の資格
出品者の所有している錦鯉で、次の各部に該当するものとす
第 1 部　15cmまで
第 2 部　15cmをこえて20cmまで
第 3 部　20cmをこえて25cmまで
第 4 部　25cmをこえて30cmまで
第 5 部　30cmをこえて35cmまで
第 6 部　35cmをこえて40cmまで
第 7 部　40cmをこえて45cmまで
第 8 部　45cmをこえて50cmまで
第 9 部　50cmをこえて55cmまで
第10部　55cmをこえて60cmまで
第11部　60cmをこえて65cmまで
第12部　65cmをこえて70cmまで
第13部　70cmをこえて75cmまで
第14部　75cmをこえて80cmまで
第15部　80cmをこえるもの

This Kohaku was the Grand Champion in the 19th All-Japan Nishikigoi Show held in Haneda, Tokyo, Japan in 1987. It is owned by Mr. Tomoaki Naito who lives in Kanagawa Prefecture in Japan. It is a huge fish, 86 cm (almost 34 inches). The judge wrote that it had strong, wide shoulders, a thick caudal peduncle and swam with a glamorous style. It had perfect balance in both behavior and in the dispersion of the red markings over the body. As with all fish in the jumbo class, the secondary sexual characteristics, such as plumpness for females and slimness for males, are not as obvious as with smaller fish. This female is not too plump because she has not been bred too much. Her red spots are large and perfectly balanced, especially on the right side. Her white skin is immaculate and noteworthy.

Mr. Shigekatsu Takahashi, who lives in Tokyo, won the Grand Prize with this Taisho Sanke. It has a magnificent Hi spot on the head which would even make a Tancho proud. This Grand Prize was awarded in the Yogyo Section, which is the section devoted to young nishikigoi. This fish is size 3.

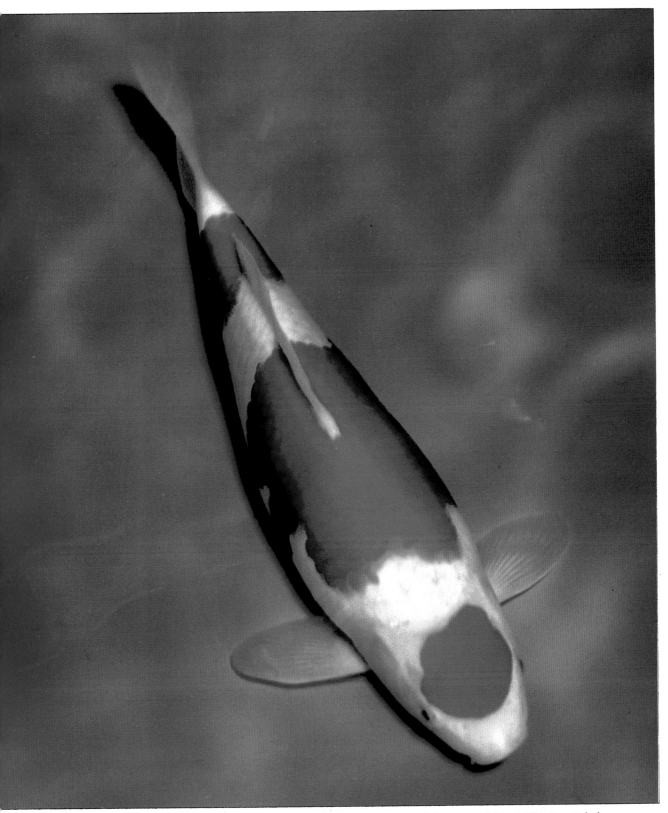

Mr. Eizo Ichiki, who lives in Chiba Prefecture, owns the Grand Prize for adolescent nishikigoi. This is a Kohaku Wakagoi (Two-color, red and white, adolescent nishikigoi) in size 4.

Mr. Tadao Katagiri owns this magnificent, almost perfect Kohaku. The large red markings could be clouds floating gently in the sky at sunset. The white is like milk. Mr. Katagiri lives in Tokyo. This fish took the Grand
Prize in the Sogyo (Adult Carp) category
in size 9.

Kazuo Ishihara, who lives in Gifu Prefecture, entered this lovely Taisho Sanke in the Seigyo (Adult Carp) category in size 12. It took the Grand Prize in this category.

Mr. Matsao Matsuda, who lives in Osaka Prefecture, took the Grand Prize in the Seigyo (Adult Carp) category for a male nishikigoi. It is a size 10 fish.

Mr. Masao Kato, of Tochigi Prefecture, won the Grand Prize in the Kyogoi (Big Carp) category. This jumbo has a size of 82 cm (more than 32 inches) and was entered in the size 25 category. This is a lovely Kohaku with three large, well-balanced patches of color.

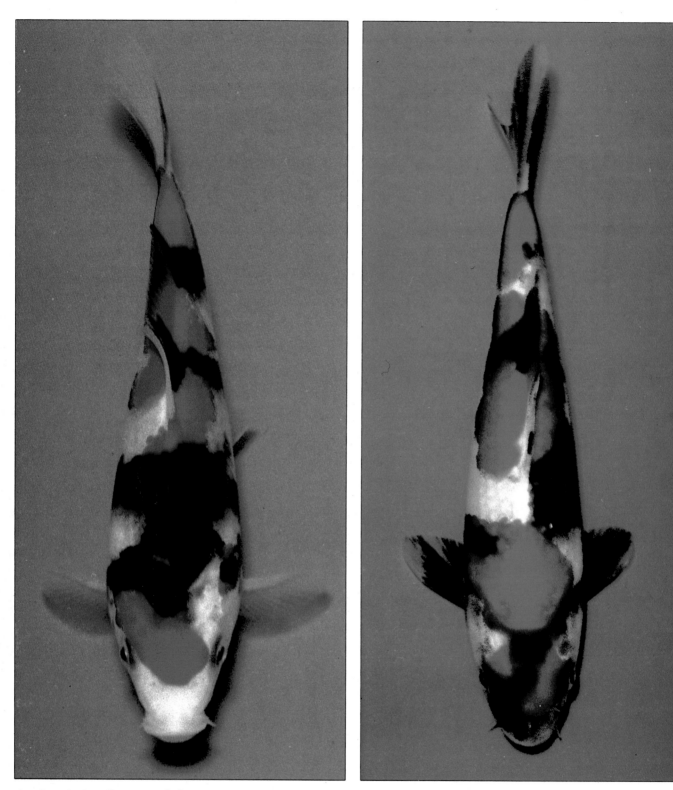

A prize-winning Showa Sanshoku in size category 1. This is very colorful for a young fish.

A very nice prize-winning Showa Sanshoku in size 2.

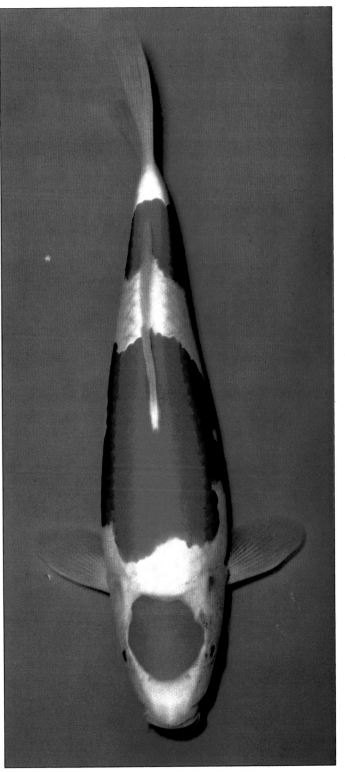

This Taisho Sanke in size 3 was a prize winner. It has an absolutely magnificent Hi spot on its head.

This lovely Kohaku with the magnificent Hi spot on its head won a prize in size 4 category.

This beautiful Kohaku won a prize in size 5 category.

This modern Showa Sanshoku is extremely well marked. It won a prize in the size 6 category.

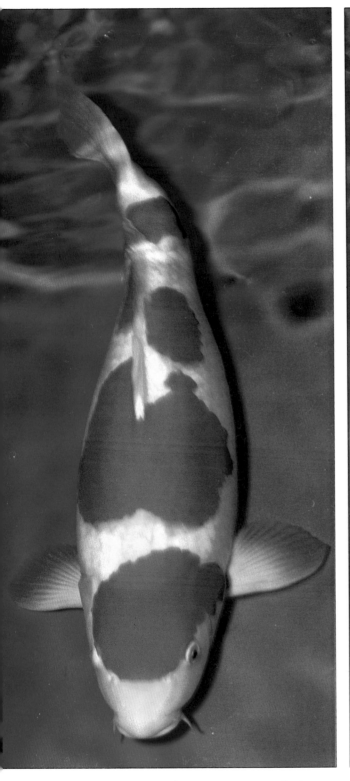

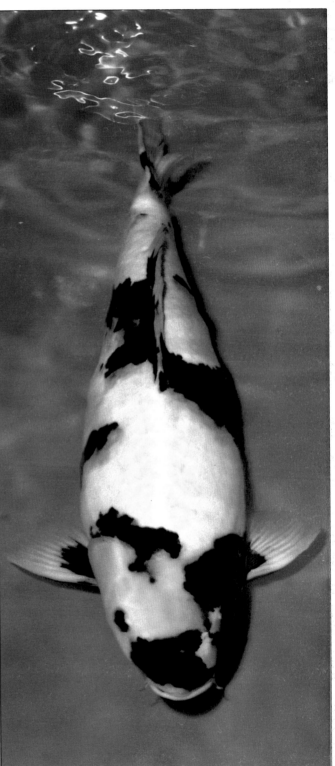

This is a magnificent Kohaku in the size 9 category. The large red marks are almost perfectly in balance on each side of the dorsal edge.

This prize-winning Shiro Utsuri in the size 10 category has very large Sumi (black) markings which make it a champion fish.

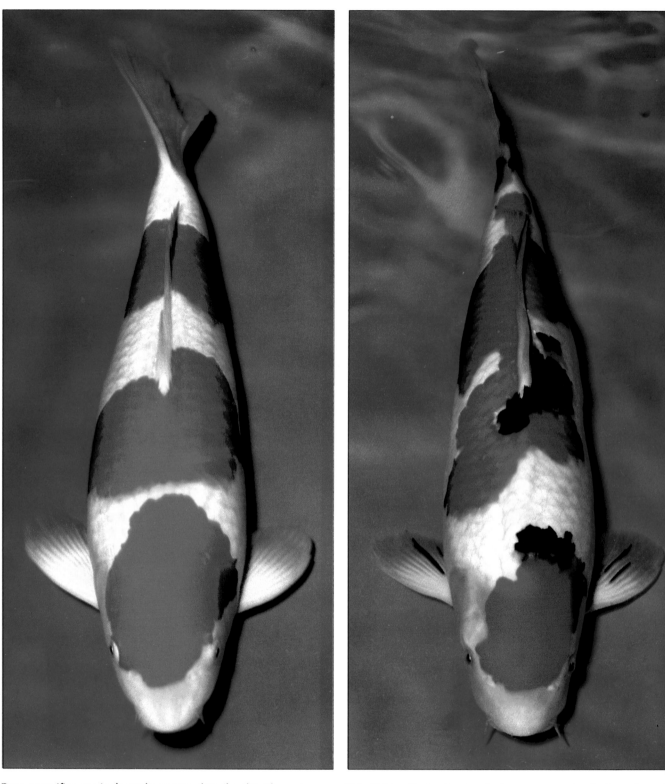

Pure magnificence is the only way to describe this Three-step Kohaku champion. Entered in the size 5 category, the very beautiful head marking is suggestive of a cloud hovering above the snow around Mount Fuji (Fujiyama).

This Taisho Sanke in size 8 shows a remarkable intrusion of the Sumi (black) patch onto the head Hi (red) spot. Ordinarily this is a demerit, but with a marking this interesting, it is admirable. This was the best Sanke in its size group, thus a champion fish.

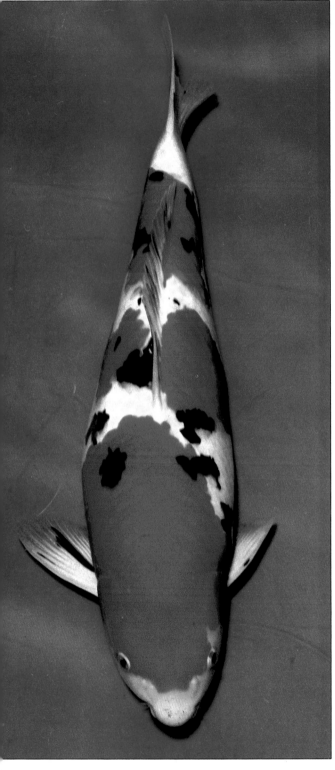

This is a highly marked Taisho Sanke. The red covers a great amount of space, while the black is intense and cleanly defined. The skin is snow white. This fish has intensity of color which the author has never seen equaled in any fish! This is a size 11 fish, about 63 cm long.

This size 12 Taisho Sanke is very nicely marked but it cannot compare with the quality of the fish to the left even though the judges gave them equal ranking.

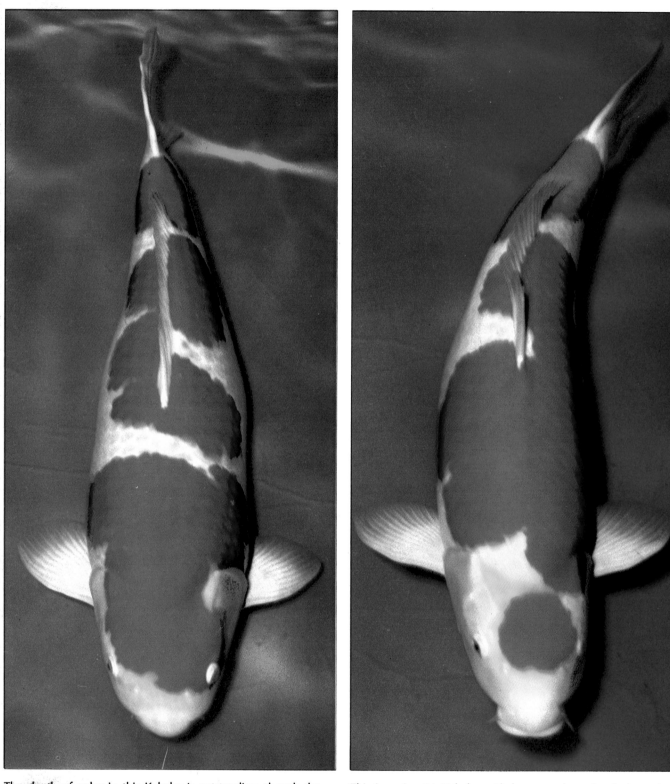

The depth of color in this Kohaku is outstanding, though the whiteness of the skin leaves something to be desired. It is nevertheless a champion fish. It belongs in size 13 category.

This is a size 14 Kohaku with large patches of red along the top of the fish which are almost connected, one to the other. It has a lovely Hi spot on the head which is barely separated from the main red color patch.

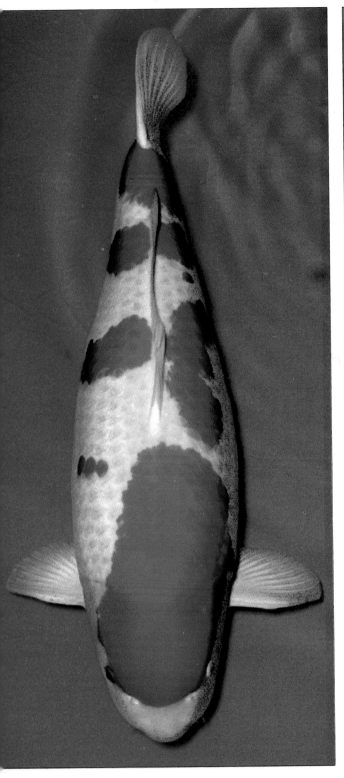

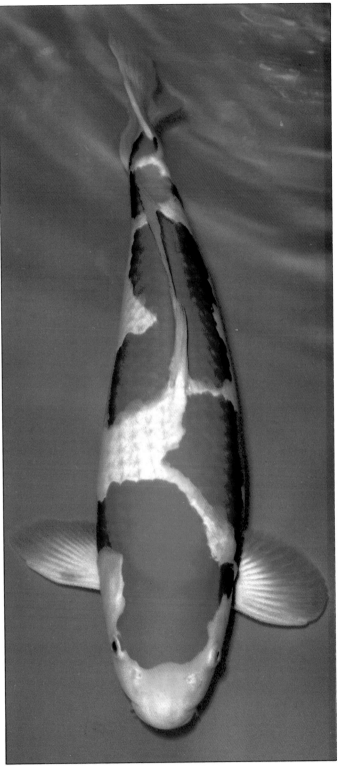

This jumbo is in category 15 which is a category of fish over 80 cm (32 inches). The size of this Kohaku is 86 cm (more than 34 inches). For its size and coloration is received a championship, but it is not a spectacular Kohaku by any means.

Compare the redness of the red and the whiteness of the white between this fish and the fish to the left. This is a younger and smaller fish, in size 9. Both are equal quality in the eyes of the Japanese judges.

This fish is a male. The fish to the left looks like a female but in such old fish, the shape is not decisive.

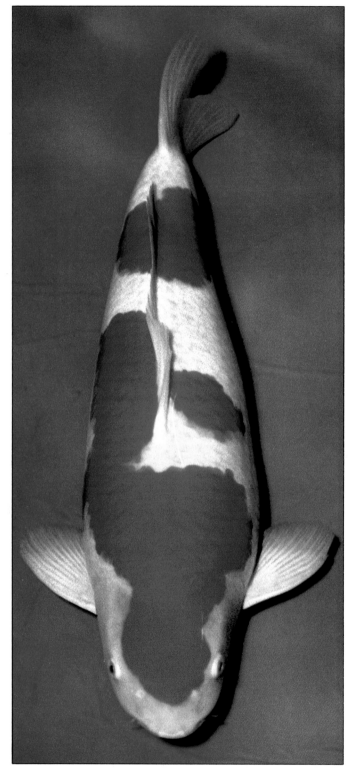

This lovely male Kohaku sports a lovely red pattern and snow white skin. It belongs to class 10 in size.

This Taisho Sanke is a champion fish because of its nice pattern of red and the delicate Sumi markings. It is a large fish in class 11, more than two feet long!

This prize-winning Kohaku has a lovely Hi spot on its head. This desirable, but rare, shape is enchanting. The fish is a size 12 which is fairly large for such a colorful fish.

The large mass of red coloring is intense and attractive. This Kohaku is in size 13, a large fish for such bright colors.

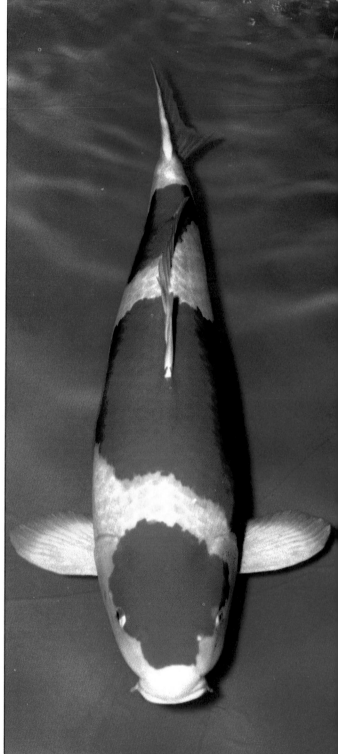

This is a nice Showa Sanshoku in size 14. It is a male, but in such an old, large fish its body bulk is deceptive.

This jumbo Kohaku is 82 cm long, so it belongs to class 15 in size. The three large red masses or steps are clearly marked and intensive. The swirling white pattern between the lovely head Hi spot and the second step is delicate and beautiful.

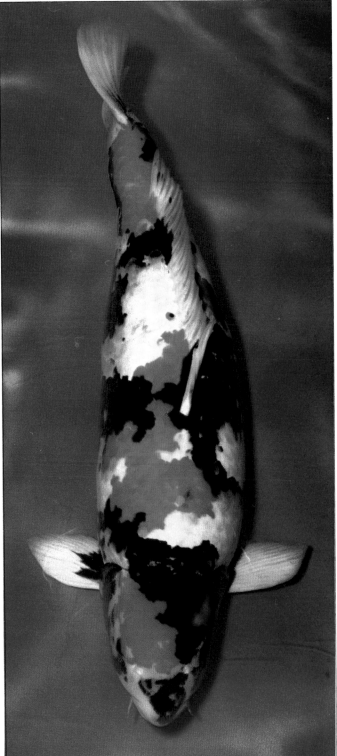

This jumbo Kohaku was 90 cm (more than 35 inches) long and weighed about 3600 grams (almost 8 pounds). It easily took first prize in the size 15 category.

This impressive Showa took first prize in the size 14 Showa Sanshoku category. It is a nicely formed male even though the bulge on the right side makes it look sick. This is merely a flexed muscle as the fish turned.

A lovely Utsuri Mono. It has an absolutely perfect body shape with perfect markings to accentuate its graceful swimming. It is a jumbo, too, in size 15. It took first prize in its category.

A Hikari Muji which took first prize in the jumbo category, size 15. The fish was 90 cm in length (more than 35 inches) and absolutely gorgeous as you can see from the photograph, The Japanese judges gave this first prize reluctantly.

The first prize Hikari Muji, size 14.

The first prize in the Asagi-Shusui category, size 11. The netting effect produced by the lighter edging on the scales is remarkable.

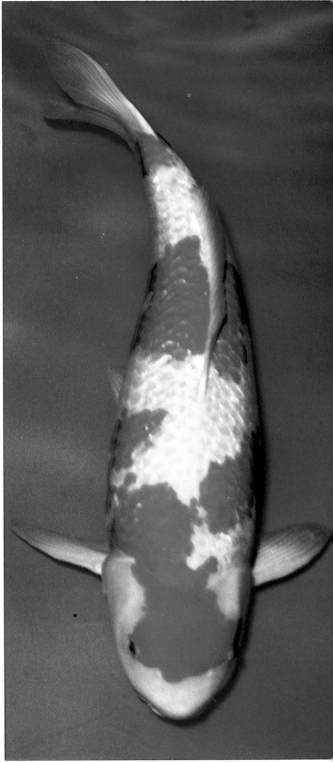

This Black Crow, Kawarimono, is neither fish nor fowl! The white lips and the slightly white marked fins hardly make it a great fish when you consider that Black Crows are found with completely white fins or white faces. However this huge fish in size 15 took a first prize. I would have preferred a solid black fish.

A Kin Gin Rin champion in size 14 with a basic Kohaku pattern and magnificently reflective scales.

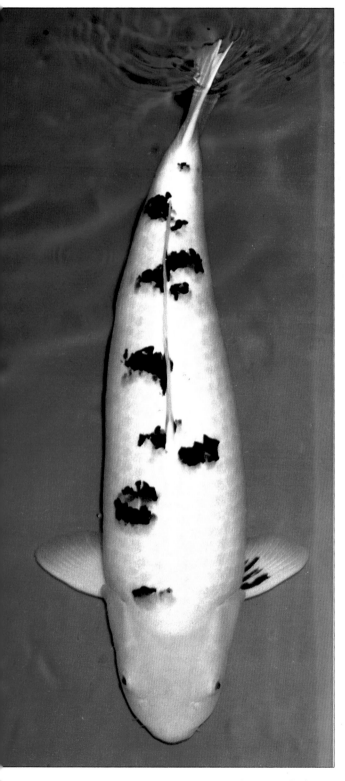

This two-color black and white fish is a Bekko. It took first prize in the size 13, Bekko category. The black is intense, like India ink, and the skin is snow white, just like it is supposed to be.

A champion Hikari Utsuri is a rare fish. This jumbo is 80 cm (more than 31 inches) just putting into the size 15 group. The weird markings over the eyes together with the nasal mask give this fish an eerie look.

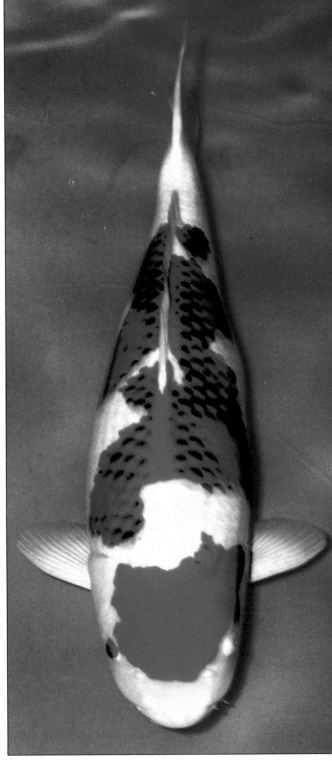

Is there anything more beautiful than a Tancho? This magnificent fish is a champion, size 12 (measuring 66 cm or 26 inches). I would have liked to see that one red scale removed but it still was the best fish in its class.

The robed beauty called Koromo is characterized by dark scales over some red scales on a basically Kohaku fish. There are black as well as blue Koromo. This is a size 12 fish of 70 cm. It is a blue Koromo.

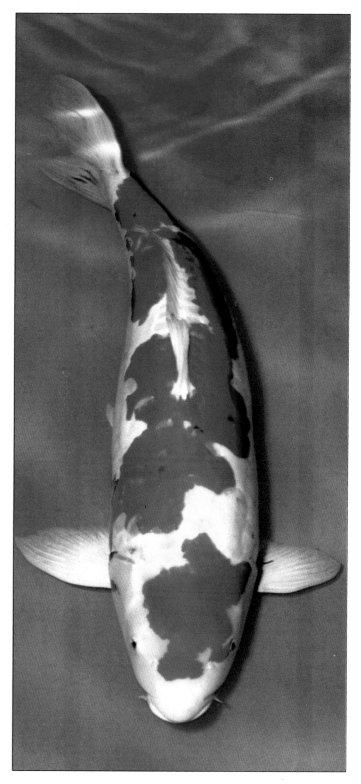

This jumbo Doitsu-goi is a magnificent Kohaku-style fish with German scales which are reflective. It measured 84 cm (33 inches) and took first prize, probably as a Gin Rin Kohaku.

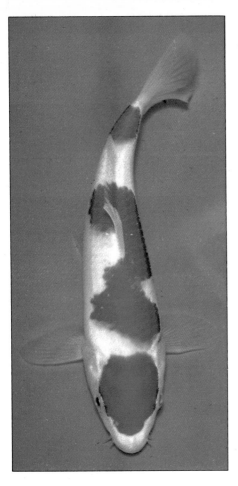
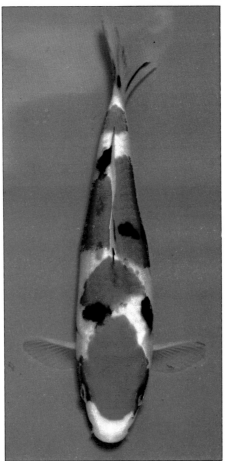

Kohaku,
Size 1

Taisho sanke,
Size 1

Utsuri Mono,
Size 1

Hikari Muji,
Size 1

Hikari Moyo,
Size 1

Asagi/Shusui,
Size 1

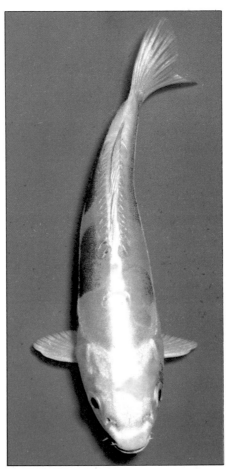

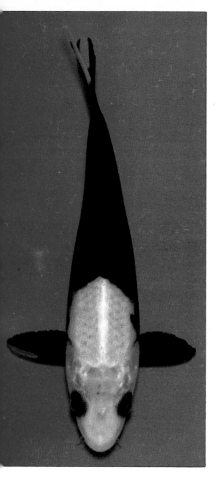

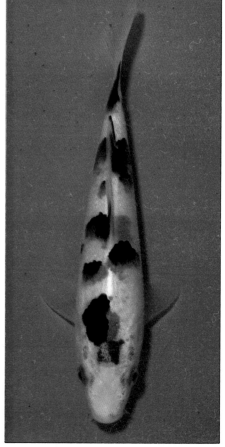

Kawarimono,
Size 1

Kin Gin Rin,
Size 1

Bekko,
Size 1

Hikari Utsuri,
Size 1

Tancho,
Size 1

Koromo,
Size 1

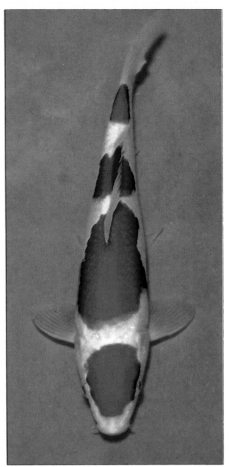

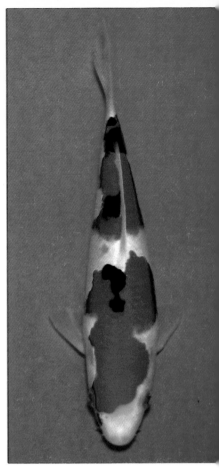

Doitsu-goi,
Size 1

Kohaku,
Size 2

Taisho sanke,
Size 2

Utsuri Mono,
Size 2

Hikari Muji,
Size 2

Hikari Moyo,
Size 2

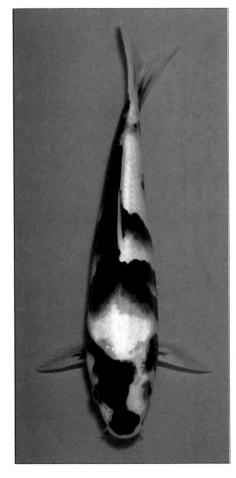

Asagi/Shusui,
Size 2

Bekko,
Size 2

Kawarimono,
Size 2

Hikari Utsuri,
Size 2

Kin Gin Rin,
Size 2

Tancho,
Size 2

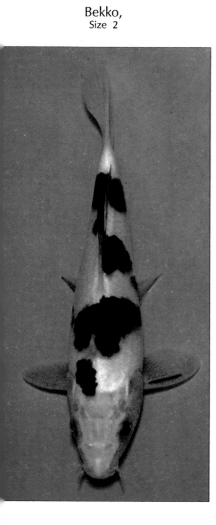

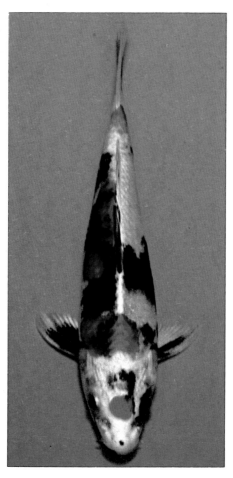

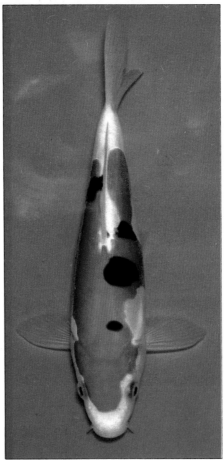

Koromo,
Size 2

Doitsu-goi,
Size 2

Kohaku,
Size 3

Showa sanke,
Size 3

Utsuri Mono,
Size 3

Hikari Muji,
Size 3

Hikari-mono,
Size 3

Asagi/Shusui,
Size 3

Kawarimono,
Size 3

Kin Gin Rin,
Size 3

Bekko,
Size 3

Hikari Utsuri,
Size 3

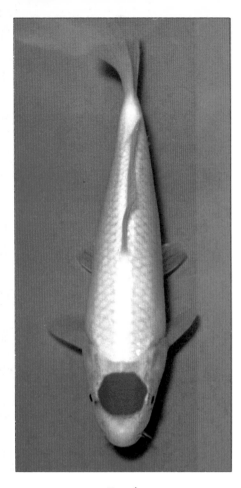

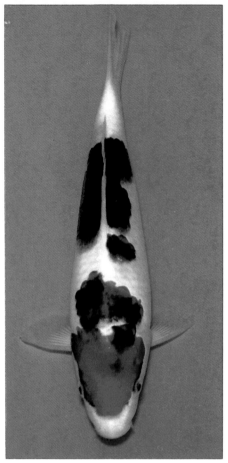

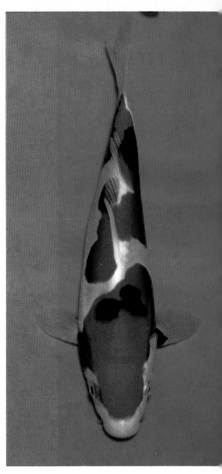

Tancho,
Size 3

Taisho sanke,
Size 4

Koromo,
Size 3

Showa sanke,
Size 4

Doitsu-goi,
Size 3

Utsuri Mono,
Size 4

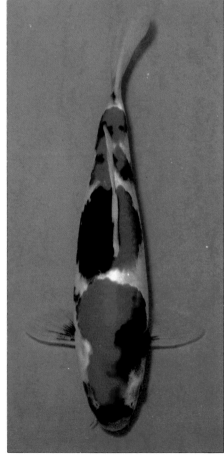

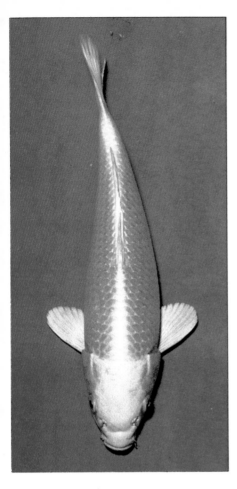

Hikari Muji,
Size 4

Hikari Moyo,
Size 4

Asagi/Shusui,
Size 4

Kawarimono,
Size 4

Kin Gin Rin,
Size 4

Bekko,
Size 4

Hikari Utsuri,
Size 4

Tancho,
Size 4

Koromo,
Size 4

Doitsu-goi,
Size 4

Taisho sanke,
Size 5

Showa sanke,
Size 5

Utsuri Mono,
Size 5

Hikari Muji,
Size 5

Hikari Moyo,
Size 5

Asagi/Shusui,
Size 5

Kawarimono,
Size 5

Kin Gin Rin,
Size 5

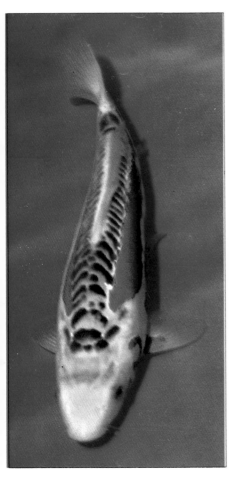

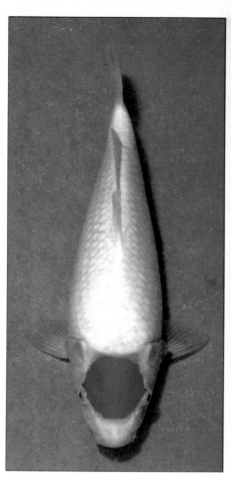

Bekko,
Size 5

Hikari Utsuri,
Size 5

Tancho,
Size 5

Koromo,
Size 5

Doitsu-goi,
Size 5

Kohaku,
Size 6

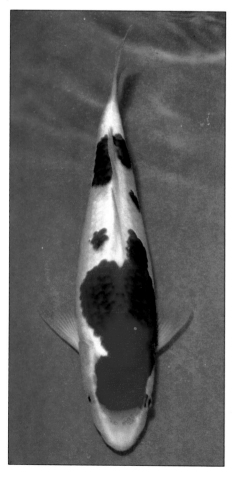

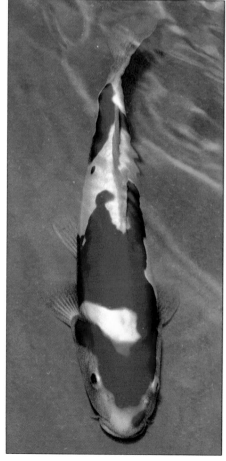

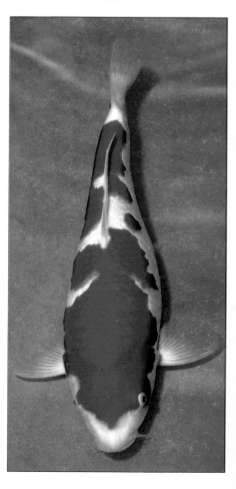

Taisho sanke,
Size 6

Utsuri Mono,
Size 6

Hikari Muji,
Size 6

Hikari Muji,
Size 6

Asagi/Shusui,
Size 6

Kawarimono,
Size 6

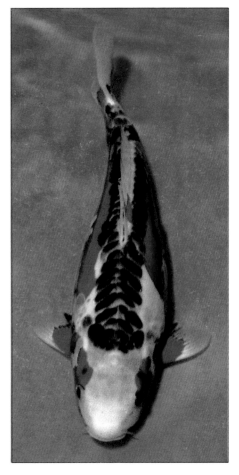

Kin Gin Rin,
Size 6

Bekko,
Size 6

Hikari Utsuri,
Size 6

Tancho,
Size 6

Koromo,
Size 6

Doitsu-goi,
Size 6

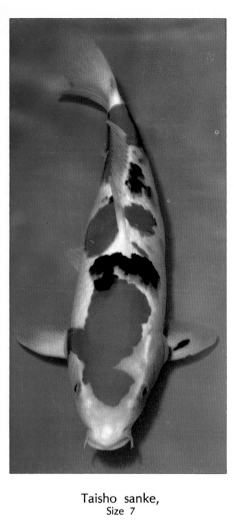

Taisho sanke,
Size 7

Showa sanke,
Size 7

Utsuri Mono,
Size 7

Hikari Muji,
Size 7

Hikari Moyo,
Size 7

Kin Gin Rin,
Size 7

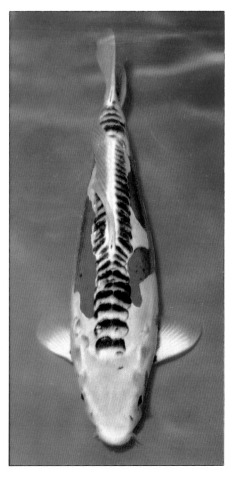

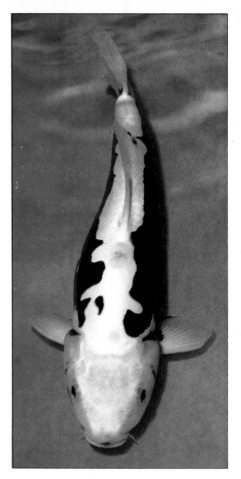

Kawarimono,
Size 7

Kin Gin Rin,
Size 7

Bekko,
Size 7

Hikari Utsuri,
Size 7

Tancho,
Size 7

Koromo,
Size 7

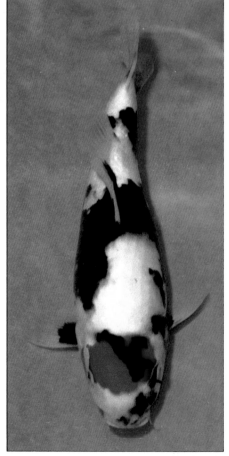

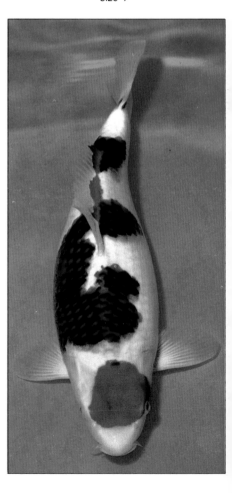

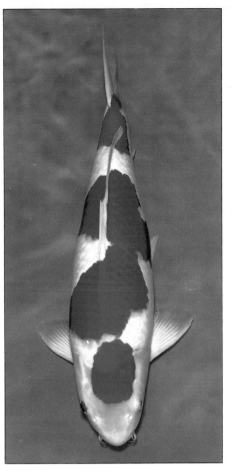

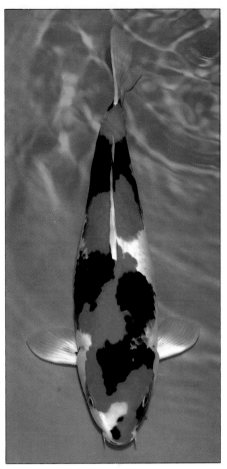

Doitsu-goi,
Size 7

Kohaku,
Size 8

Showa sanke,
Size 8

Utsuri Mono,
Size 8

Hikari Muji,
Size 8

Hikari Moyo,
Size 8

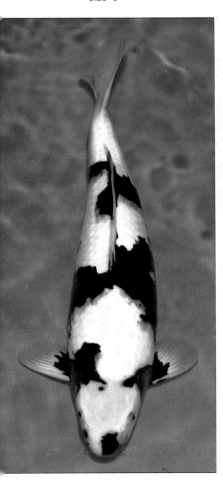

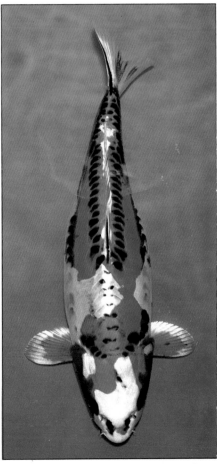

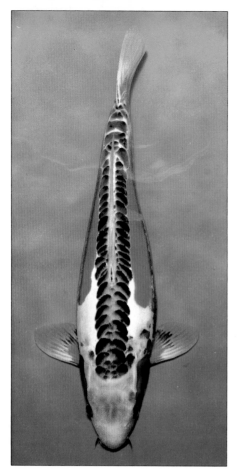

Asagi/Shusui,
Size 8

Bekko,
Size 8

Kawarimono,
Size 8

Hikari Utsuri,
Size 8

Kin Gin Rin,
Size 8

Tancho,
Size 8

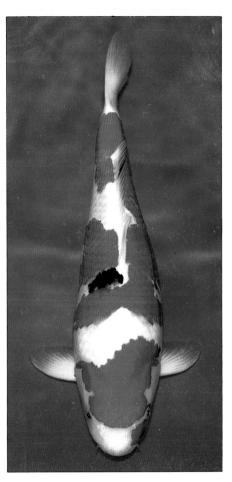

Koromo,
Size 8

Doitsu-goi,
Size 8

Taisho sanke,
Size 9

Showa sanke,
Size 9

Utsuri Mono,
Size 9

Hikari Muji,
Size 9

Hikari Moyo,
Size 9

Asagi/Shusui,
Size 9

Kawarimono,
Size 9

Kin Gin Rin,
Size 9

Bekko,
Size 9

Hikari Utsuri,
Size 9

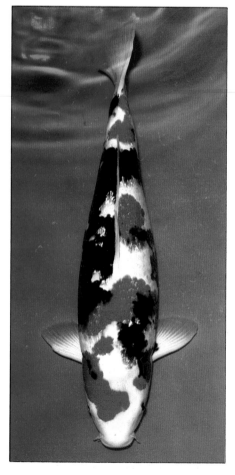

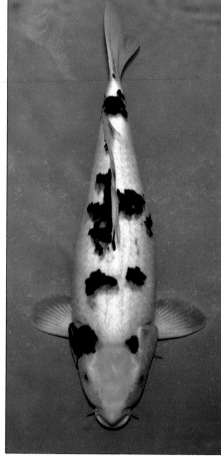

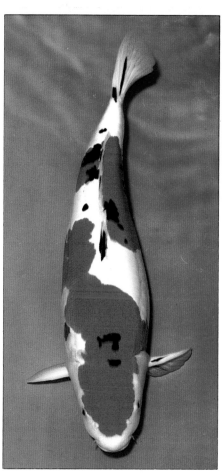

Tancho,
Size 9

Koromo,
Size 9

Doitsu-goi,
Size 9

Kohaku,
Size 10

Taisho sanke,
Size 10

Showa sanke,
Size 10

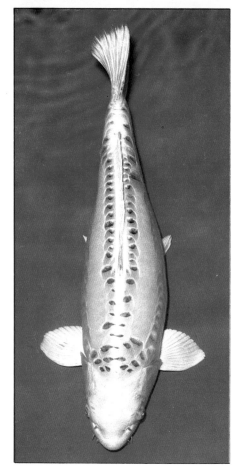

Hikari Muji,
Size 10

Kawarimono,
Size 10

Hikari Moyo,
Size 10

Kin Gin Rin,
Size 10

Asagi/Shusui,
Size 10

Bekko,
Size 10

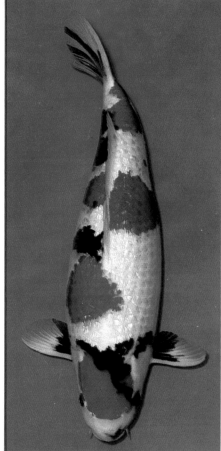

Hikari Utsuri,
Size 10

Tancho,
Size 10

Koromo,
Size 10

Doitsu-goi,
Size 10

Kohaku,
Size 11

Showa sanke,
Size 11

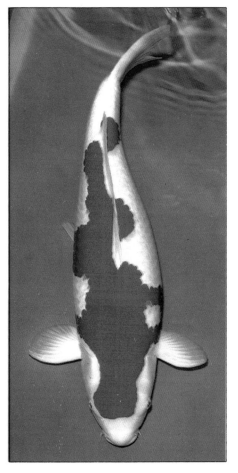

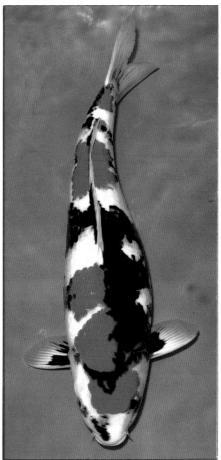

Utsuri Mono,
Size 11

Hikari Muji,
Size 11

Hikari Moyo,
Size 11

Kawarimono,
Size 11

Kin Gin Rin,
Size 11

Bekko,
Size 11

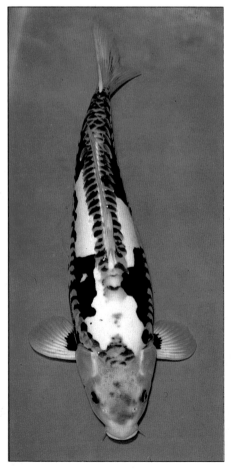

Hikari Utsuri,
Size 11

Tancho,
Size 11

Koromo,
Size 11

Doitsu-goi,
Size 11

Kohaku,
Size 12

Showa sanke,
Size 12

Utsuri Mono,
Size 12

Asagi/Shusui,
Size 12

Hikari Muji,
Size 12

Kawarimono,
Size 12

Hikari Moyo,
Size 12

Kin Gin Rin,
Size 12

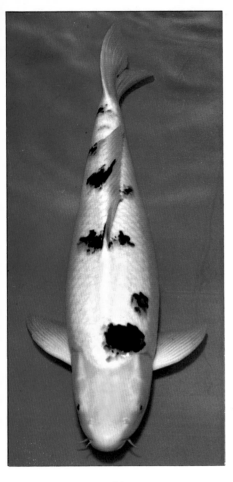

Bekko,
Size 12

Hikari Utsuri,
Size 12

Doitsu-goi,
Size 12

Taisho sanke,
Size 13

Showa sanke,
Size 13

Utsuri Mono,
Size 13

Hikari Muji,
Size 13

Hikari Moyo,
Size 13

Asagi/Shusui,
Size 13

Kawarimono,
Size 13

Kin Gin Rin,
Size 13

Hikari Utsuri,
Size 13

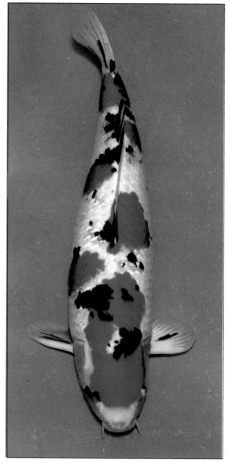

Tancho,
Size 13

Showa sanke,
Size 14

Koromo,
Size 13

Showa sanke,
Size 14

Doitsu-goi,
Size 13

Utsuri Mono,
Size 14

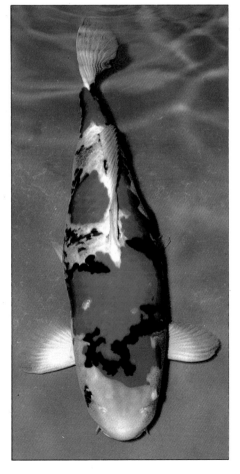

Hikari Muji,
Size 14

Hikari Moyo,
Size 14

Asagi/Shusui,
Size 14

Kawarimono,
Size 14

Bekko,
Size 14

Hikari Utsuri,
Size 14

Tancho,
Size 14

Taisho sanke,
Size 15

Koromo,
Size 14

Showa sanke,
Size 15

Doitsu-goi,
Size 14

Asagi/Shusui,
Size 15

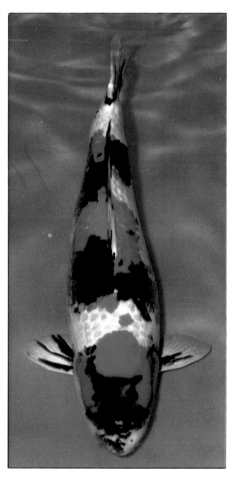

Koromo,
Size 15

Taisho sanke,
Size 9

Showa-utsuri,
Size 9

Utsuri Mono,
Size 9

Kawarimono,
Size 9

Doitsu-goi,
Size 9

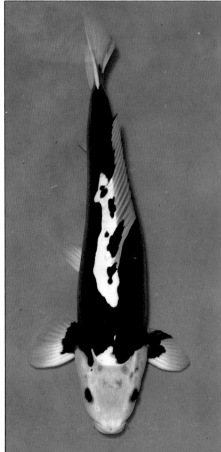

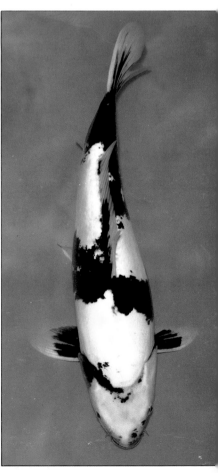

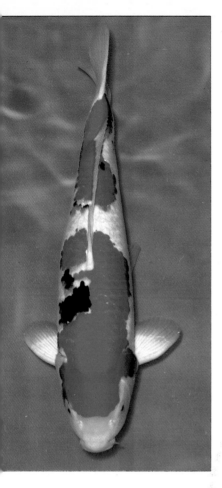

Taisho sanke,
Size 10

Shiro-utsuri,
Size 10

Utsuri Mono,
Size 10

Kawarimono,
Size 10

Kohaku,
Size 11

Showa-utsuri,
Size 11

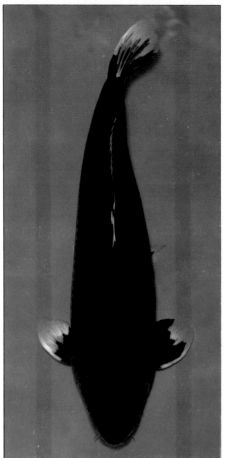

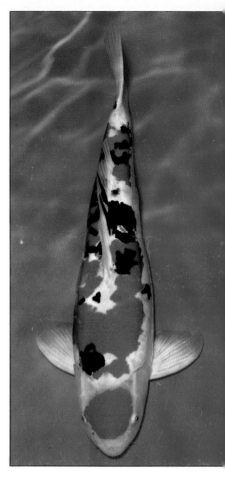

Hikari-mono,
Size 11

Taisho sanke,
Size 12

Kawarimono,
Size 11

Showa-utsuri,
Size 12

Doitsu-goi,
Size 11

Kawarimono,
Size 12

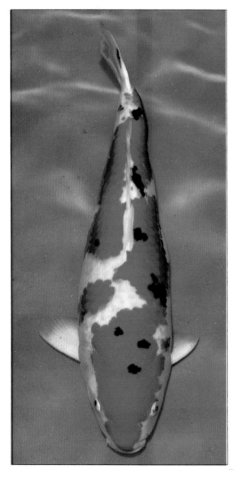

Doitsu-goi,
Size 12

Taisho sanke,
Size 13

Showa-utsuri,
Size 13

Hikari-mono,
Size 13

Kawarimonò,
Size 13

Doitsu-goi,
Size 14

Kohaku,
Size 1

Taisho sanke,
Size 1

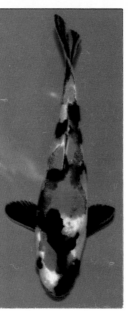

Showa sanke,
Size 1

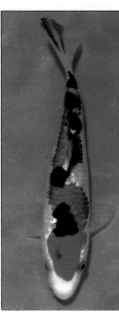

Kin Gin Rin,
Size 1

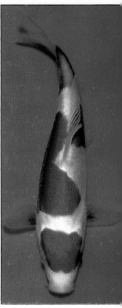

Doitsu-goi,
Size 1

Kohaku,
Size 2

Taisho sanke,
Size 2

Showa sanke,
Size 2

Kin Gin Rin,
Size 2

Kohaku,
Size 3

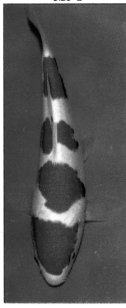

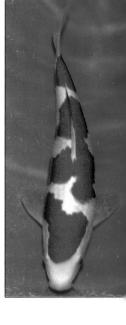

Taisho sanke,
Size 3

Showa sanke,
Size 3

Kin Gin Rin,
Size 3

Kohaku,
Size 4

Taisho sanke,
Size 4

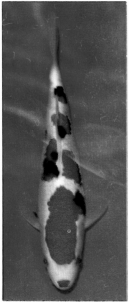

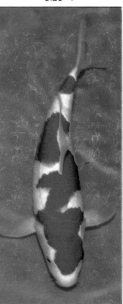

Showa sanke,
Size 4
Taisho sanke,
Size 5

Utsuri Mono,
Size 4
Showa sanke,
Size 5

Kin Gin Rin,
Size 4
Utsuri Mono,
Size 5

Doitsu-goi,
Size 4
Kin Gin Rin,
Size 5

Kohaku,
Size 5
Kohaku,
Size 6

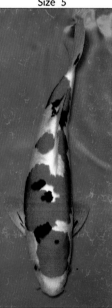

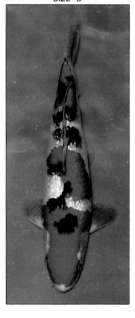
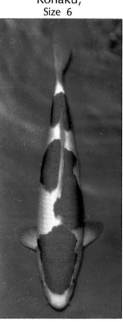

Taisho sanke,
Size 6

Showa sanke,
Size 6

Showa sanke,
Size 6

Kin Gin Rin,
Size 6

Kohaku,
Size 7

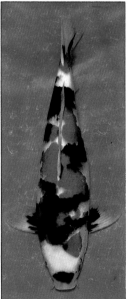

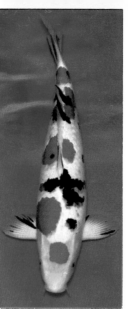

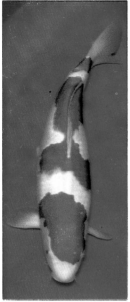

Kohaku,
Size 7

Kohaku,
Size 7

Taisho sanke,
Size 7

Showa sanke,
Size 7

Kin Gin Rin,
Size 7

Doitsu-goi,
Size 7

Kohaku,
Size 8

Kohaku,
Size 8

Kohaku,
Size 8

Taisho sanke,
Size 8

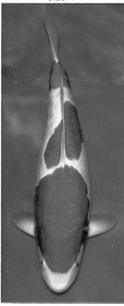
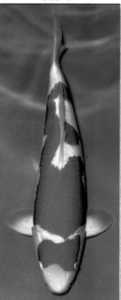

Taisho sanke,
Size 8

Showa sanke,
Size 8

Showa sanke,
Size 8

Kin Gin Rin,
Size 8

Kohaku,
Size 9

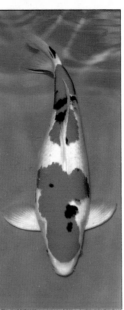

Kohaku,
Size 9
Kohaku,
Size 10

Taisho sanke,
Size 9
Kohaku,
Size 10

Taisho sanke,
Size 9
Kohaku,
Size 10

Showa sanke,
Size 9
Taisho sanke,
Size 10

Utsuri Mono,
Size 9
Showa sanke,
Size 10

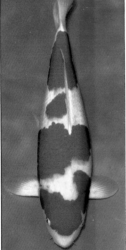
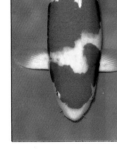

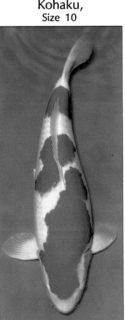

Utsuri Mono,
Size 10

Kin Gin Rin,
Size 10

Kohaku,
Size 11

Taisho sanke,
Size 11

Taisho sanke,
Size 11

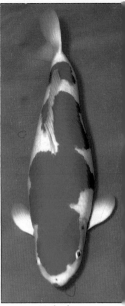

Showa sanke,
Size 11
Kohaku,
Size 12

Utsuri Mono,
Size 11
Kohaku,
Size 12

Utsuri Mono,
Size 11
Taisho sanke,
Size 12

Kawarimono,
Size 11
Taisho sanke,
Size 12

Kohaku,
Size 12
Taisho sanke,
Size 12

Showa sanke,
Size 12

Utsuri Mono,
Size 12

Utsuri Mono,
Size 12

Utsuri Mono,
Size 12

Kohaku,
Size 13

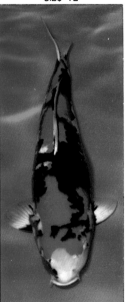

Kohaku,
Size 13
Taisho sanke,
Size 14

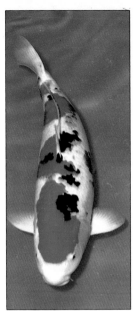

Taisho sanke,
Size 13
Showa sanke,
Size 14

Taisho sanke,
Size 13
Kawarimono,
Size 14

Utsuri Mono,
Size 13
Kohaku,
Size 15

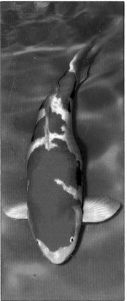

Kohaku,
Size 14
Taisho sanke,
Size 15

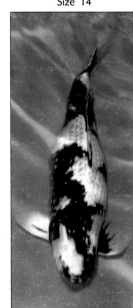

Showa sanke,
Size 15

Utsuri Mono,
Size 15

Kohaku,
Size 9
Showa-utsuri,
Size 10

Taisho sanke,
Size 9
Kohaku,
Size 11

Showa sanke,
Size 9
Kohaku,
Size 11

Kohaku,
Size 10
Kohaku,
Size 12

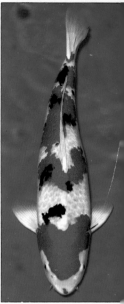

Taisho sanke,
Size 10
Kohaku,
Size 12

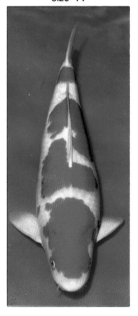

Showa sanke,
Size 13

SCENES FROM THE 19th ALL-JAPAN NISHIKIGOI SHOW
The judges are evaluating the entries.

SCENES FROM THE 19TH ALL-JAPAN NISHIKIGOI SHOW
Winners and their prizes.

SCENES FROM THE 19TH ALL-JAPAN NISHIKIHGOI
SHOW.
There were 3,585 fish entered into the competition.

141

第19回 国魚の祭典 全日本総合錦鯉品評会

第19回 国魚の祭典 全日本総合錦鯉品評会

第19回 国魚の祭典 全日本総合錦鯉品評会

第19回 国魚の祭典 全日本総合錦鯉品評会

第19回 国魚の祭典 全日本総合錦鯉品評会

SCENES FROM THE 19TH ALL-JAPAN NISHIKIGOI SHOW
These show the teams of judges and workers responsible for
putting on the exhibition.

Suggested Reading

The following books by T.F.H. Publications are available at pet shops everywhere.

KOI OF THE WORLD—
Japanese Colored Carp
By Dr. Herbert R. Axelrod
ISBN 0-87666-092-8
T.F.H. #H-947
Until the publication of *Koi Varieties,* this book was far and away the most up-to-date and colorful book about koi in the English language. Covering such important topics as the basic needs of koi, breeding koi, koi diseases, fish sales and koi shows, the book is loaded with excellent big full-color photos of different koi varieties, all properly identified. This is the first English-language text ever to capture the romance of koi and make it understandable to Occidental eyes. Big and beautiful and still a great value.
Hard cover, 9 x 12", 240 pages
Contains 327 full-color photos, 27 black and white photos

KOI AND GARDEN PONDS:
A Complete Introduction
By Dr. Herbert R. Axelrod
Hardcover **CO-040** ISBN 0-86622-398-3
Softcover **CO-040S** ISBN 0-86622-399-1
For anyone interested in the Japanese carp and for owners of garden pools. This is a truly beautiful book with great value as an identifier of the many different scale and color patterns of koi.
5½ x 8½, 96 pages
Contains 104 full-color photos and 108 full-color line drawings.

GARDEN PONDS: A Complete Introduction
By Al David
Hardcover **CO-017** ISBN 0-86622-266-9
Softcover **CO-017S** ISBN 0-86622-298-7
This highly colorful book shows and tells readers how to set up a garden pond or pool. Authoritative advice is given about making the pond, how to protect it against enemies, which fish and plants to put into it—and how to keep it beautiful.
5½ x 8½, 96 pages
Contains 114 full-color photos and 22 full-color line drawings

GENETICS FOR THE AQUARIST
By Dr. J. Schroder
ISBN 0-87666-461-3
TFH PS-656
This is the only book in the English language that deals entirely with the genetics of fish kept as pets. Invaluable for an understanding of trait inheritance in fish.
Soft Cover, 5½ x8", 125 pages
10 black and white photos, 59 color photos, 30 line drawings, 12 tables.

WATER GARDENS FOR PLANTS AND FISH
By Charles B. Thomas
ISBN 0-866232-942-6
TS-102
Highly illustrated with full-color photos, plus full-color diagrams and diagnostic drawings, this book has been written by one of the world's foremost commercial water gardeners. It concentrates on providing practical advice about setting up a garden pond and keeping it beautiful. Easy to read and highly useful.
Hardcover 5½ x 8, 192 pages

TEXTBOOK OF FISH HEALTH
By Dr. George W. Post
ISBN 0-87666-599-7
T.F.H. H-1043
Owners of expensive fish like koi need a good understanding of how fish become ill, and this book is a complete account of all of the mechanisms and organisms that cause diseases in fishes, with emphasis on the diseases of bacterial and viral origin. Covers history, signs, treatment and distribution. Illustrated with hundreds of full-color photos that are excellent aids in the identification of diseases and their causes.
For scientists, hobbyists, fish culturists, students. College level.

Index

Page numbers in **bold** refer to photographs.